THE PAST IN PERSPECTIVE

Series Editors: C. C. Eldridge and Ralph A. Griffiths

DEMOCRACY IN A DEPRESSION

THE PAST IN PERSPECTIVE

Series Editors: C. C. Eldridge and Ralph A. Griffiths

C. C. Eldridge is Reader in History at the University of Wales, Lampeter.

Ralph A. Griffiths is Professor of Medieval History at the University of Wales, Swansea.

Other titles in this series:

THE PAST IN PERSPECTIVE

DEMOCRACY IN A DEPRESSION

BRITAIN IN THE 1920s AND 1930s

Malcolm Smith

CARDIFF
UNIVERSITY OF WALES PRESS
1998

© Malcolm Smith, 1998

British Library Cataloguing-In-Publication Data.
A catalogue record for this book is available from the British
Library.

ISBN (paperback) 0-7083-1448-1
       (cased) 0-7083-1449-X

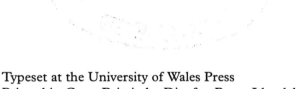

Typeset at the University of Wales Press
Printed in Great Britain by Dinefwr Press, Llandybïe

Contents

Editors' Foreword

Each volume in this series, *The Past in Perspective*, deals with a major theme of British, European or World history. The aim of the series is to engage the interest of all for whom knowledge of the riches of the world's historical experience is a delight, and in particular to meet the needs of students of history in universities and colleges – and at comparatively modest cost.

Each theme is tackled at sufficient length and in sufficient depth to allow each writer both to advance our understanding of the subject in the light of the most recent research, and to place his or her approach in due perspective. Accordingly, each volume contains a historiographical chapter which assesses how interpretations of its theme have developed, and have been criticized, endorsed, modified or discarded. Each volume, too, includes a section of substantial excerpts from key original sources: this reflects the importance of allowing the reader to come to his or her own conclusions about differing interpretations, and also the greater accessibility nowadays of original sources in print. Furthermore, in each volume there is a detailed bibliography which not only underpins the writer's own account and analysis, but also enables the reader to pursue the theme, or particular aspects of it, to even greater depth; the explosion of historical writing in the twentieth century makes such guidance invaluable. By these perspectives, taken together, each volume is an up-to-date, authoritative and substantial exploration of themes, ancient, medieval or modern, of British, European, American or World significance, after more than a century of the study and teaching of history.

C. C. Eldridge and Ralph A. Griffiths

Explanatory note
References to the Illustrative Documents which follow the main text

are indicated by a bold roman numeral preceded by the word 'DOCUMENT', all within square brackets [**DOCUMENT XII**].

Acknowledgements

The author and publishers wish to thank the following for kind permission to reproduce extracts in this volume:

Document XII: Random House for the extract from *English Journey* by J. B. Priestley originally published by Penguin

Document XVIII: Crown copyright material in the Public Record Office is reproduced by permission of the Controller of Her Majesty's Stationery Office (CAB 53/41, no. COS765)

Every effort has been made to trace the copyright holders of substantial extracts in this volume. In the case of any queries, please contact the publishers.

1. Historians and the Depression

It is no less the truth for being a cliché that history is a never-ending story. The particular significance of this in the case of recent history is that the end of the story, the present, keeps throwing a different perspective on events in the past. In a novel or a film, events assume full significance only in the light of subsequent events, and can only be fully understood at the end of the narrative. In the case of history – one hopes at least – there is no final end to the story. Consequently, we are always in the process of plot development, reassessing events that led to the current, but ever-changing, end of the story. The history of Britain between the wars has been one of very distinct shifts of emphasis. This has not been, primarily at least, because we have come to know a great deal more about the period as time has moved on. Certainly, the opening of the public records for virtually the whole of the inter-war period, in 1967, made available a wealth of material which helped historians to build a more detailed picture of the issues at stake. There were, however, few major revelations, just more detail. New interpretation has tended to come not from new facts as such but from new angles of vision, approaches to the facts.

In his *English History, 1914–1945*, A. J. P. Taylor pointed out the difficulty of judging the comparative significance of these two facts about the 1930s: that there were never fewer than one million unemployed, and that one million new cars came on to the roads. In the age of welfare politics of the 1950s and 1960s, the unemployment rate of the decade was the dominant and appalling fact. In the consumerist 1970s and 1980s, the picture of the 1930s as the beginning of the contemporary economy came to dominate. The most dominant fact of all about the inter-war period, perhaps, is that it has continued to have immense political significance until very recently. There are, moreover, so many paradoxes about Britain's experience of the depression years that it is possible credibly to put forward interpretations which are wholly at odds with each other.

Which one has held good and become mainstream has depended on the shifts in the political climate since the period ended.

Guilty men and people's war

The inter-war period began to be evaluated as soon as it was over, and the initial reckoning was a bitter one. The coming of the Second World War neatly sandwiched the 1920s and the 1930s as 'inter-war', as an interlude between two major world crises and, inevitably therefore, as a time of failure or, at best, of standing still. On the day Hitler invaded Poland, the poet W. H. Auden famously branded the 1930s 'the low dishonest decade', the years in which Fascism had flourished and the world had drifted into another war, the years of the dole queues, hunger marches and the humiliation of the working class. Journalism contributed to popular political rhetoric a series of deftly packaged images and phrases: these had been 'the locust years', 'the hungry thirties', 'the devil's decade'. While the 1920s got away relatively lightly, as a period merely of irresponsibility and hedonism – the 'roaring twenties' – the thirties attracted universal condemnation. Central to this demonization of the period, understandably perhaps in 1940 as Britain appeared on the brink of military defeat, was the appeasement of Nazi Germany and the lack of military preparation that allegedly went with appeasement. In that year, three journalists working for Beaverbrook newspapers, Michael Foot, Frank Owen and Peter Howard, published a vitriolic personal attack on those responsible for appeasement and, in particular, on Neville Chamberlain. The book was called *Guilty Men*. Avowedly present-orientated in its use of history, the front cover featured a quotation from Winston Churchill, the new prime minister: 'the point of recriminating about the past is to enforce action in the present.' *Guilty Men* opened on the beaches of Dunkirk and traced that disaster back to the lack of military preparation, the absurd optimism of the appeasers and their blind acceptance of Hitler's mantra: 'we have no territorial demands to make in Europe'. **[DOCUMENT I]** The book ended by demanding the sacking of the 'guilty men' as clear evidence that the government was fully committed to the fight.

In fact, Neville Chamberlain was to die before the year was out. Others in the Cabinets of the 1930s were to be sidelined into relatively unimportant jobs. Only Kingsley Wood survived his association with appeasement to stay on in high office, but he too was to die before the end of the war. Stanley Baldwin's status as a guilty man was to be confirmed by the furious press reaction to his unwillingness to surrender the iron railings of his country house for the wartime scrap-metal drive. In the 1950s, 'Rab' Butler did not achieve his ambition of the premiership, perhaps because of his association with appeasement. Neither did Alec Douglas-Home ever fully recover from the stigma of being the man who had actually handed to Chamberlain in the House of Commons Hitler's invitation to the Munich conference, and who had stood behind the prime minister in the famous newsreel of Chamberlain waving the 'piece of paper' on his return. [**DOCUMENT II**] Even when he was foreign and commonwealth secretary dealing decades later with the unilateral declaration of independence by Rhodesia-Zimbabwe, the taunt of appeasement could be thrown at him by the Opposition. The generation of Conservative politicians that appeased Hitler in the 1930s was blighted by that policy for the rest of their careers. *Guilty Men* may not have been a scholarly piece but its tone of moral outrage was to be typical of historical attitudes towards appeasement until the 1970s.

Two other rapid assessments of the inter-war years were to feature on university reading lists into the 1960s and were equally critical in their tone. Neither of them was written by a professional historian. Malcolm Muggeridge's *The Thirties* was a witty lampooning of the pretensions of Britain's leaders between the wars which concentrated again almost entirely on foreign policy. Muggeridge's story was primarily a moral one, of the decline of values. This was a chronicle of failed leadership, of pomposity and materialism, typical of the view of the world of 'St Mug', part world-weary, part apocalyptic. At the same time, Robert Graves and Alan Hodge rushed out *The Long Weekend* which, as the title suggests, viewed the inter-war years as a period of abstention from reality, a holiday from the workaday world of global war which preceded and succeeded it. In Graves's and Hodge's rendition, the twenties were a time of optimism, of potential for social and political transformation after the war to end wars, but these hopes had been snuffed out by the thirties, characterized as a time of befuddled and dishonest leadership. This lack of leadership in turn reflected on the people themselves, who had allowed themselves to be misled, with their zany interests in things like pacifism, nudism and hiking.

What was presented in these journalistic accounts was a pastiche of the previous twenty years, but one which appears to have been extraordinarily effective as a destruction of the reputation of leading British politicians. MacDonald, Baldwin and Chamberlain emerged as the three wise monkeys. Churchill, implicitly, emerged as the man of the hour, the only man who had foreseen the danger of Hitler, who had railed against appeasement, who had been cast into the political wilderness, and who had finally been called upon to 'save England'. This was a view of the transition from the thirties to the forties which Churchill himself was to underline, of course, in his own vastly popular semi-autobiographical history of the period written after the war. Increasingly, however, what went along with this demonization of the 'guilty men' was a sense of a new commitment to social amelioration. The new intellectual, artistic and journalistic establishment which came to dominate in the early years of the war, broadly left-wing in its political leanings, constantly referred back to the 'locust years' as the point of departure for a 'people's war'. The 'people's war' was being fought not only against Fascism and for social democracy, but also for full employment, better housing and equality of opportunity. When George Orwell announced his conversion to patriotism in 1940, in his essay 'My country right or left', he presaged the temporary capture of the patriotic mantle by the left in Britain. Only 'idiots' had failed to foresee the present war, he declared, and 'only revolution can save England, and now it has begun.' By 1945, the electorate could cheer for Churchill but vote his party into opposition, as the remnants of the 'guilty men'. It had become virtually a patriotic duty to rail against the thirties and those who had led the country to international dishonour, and had led the people through social misery.

The inter-war years and the post-war years

The powerful ideological machinery which, by 1945, had set the 1940s against the 1930s, the National Governments of the pre-war years against the wartime coalition, was to dominate political culture in Britain for a generation. When historians came to write up the inter-war years in the 1950s and 1960s, after that passage of time which historians often feel is necessary to gain perspective, they could hardly help but be affected by the climate of the post-war years. Charles Mowat, in the preface to his enormously influential *Britain between the Wars* (1955), accepted that 'any work of this kind is bound to be, in some sort and however unwittingly, autobiographical', but he felt that he could 'profit from the perspective afforded by some lapse of time and the interposition of the Second World War'. In fact, the Second World War had limited rather than broadened perspectives. Britain was locked into the ideas of Beveridge and Keynes, the basis of the post-war political settlement: these ideas involved a specific rejection of those ideas which were now deemed to have dominated the inter-war years.

Mowat's history is one of despondency bounded by hope. The book begins with President Woodrow Wilson's hopes in 1918 that people would see an age brightening from decade to decade, but prepares the reader for what is to follow: 'the history of the twenty years between the two world wars is the history of the disappointment of these hopes'. In the last paragraph of the book, a subsection entitled 'Alone', hope returns for the British people: 'In the summer of 1940, as they awaited the Battle of Britain, they found themselves again, after twenty years of indecision. They turned away from past regrets and faced the future unafraid.' The inter-war years are presented as a depressing voyage of rediscovery, a kind of vale of tears between Britain's age of imperialism and Britain's age of welfarism. Mowat's is largely, although by no means wholly, a political history. The set pieces are the political retrenchment which put an end to post-war hopes by 1922. The turning-point is the series of events leading up to the political crisis of 1931, and the last two chapters, of a total of eleven, are on appeasement. There are only two chapters on the social and cultural 'condition of Britain', one to counterpoint each of the political histories of the twenties and the thirties. But these chapters are actually enormously important in Mowat's narrative. It is in the second of these chapters, 'The secret people and the social conscience', that the hope for the future emerges in the thirties, in the shape of new technology, modern housing estates and a restless, young liberal intelligentsia dissatisfied with the dominant political norms and galvanized by the Fascist threat. While the political history of the inter-war period was one of failure, Mowat implies, an alternative was emerging from the new social fabric to point to the future. The phrase 'secret people' was a reference to a poem by G. K. Chesterton which had suggested that the silent nation would soon make its voice heard on the folly of its leaders.

Mowat provided the classic model for historical thinking about the inter-war years as a period of aimlessness between two ages of very different certainties. This model was dominated by politics, specifically political failure by both mainstream right and left to grasp the problem of the depression firmly by the horns. This failure of vision in economic and in social policy was compounded by an utter lack of will when it came to the foreign threat. In the meantime, the younger intelligentsia provided an alternative road to the future which the collapse of the Chamberlain government in 1940 allowed to emerge, a modernist and forward-looking commitment to planning and to social conscience to replace the faded remnants of Edwardian *laissez-faire*.

Arthur Marwick gave firmer shape to the development of this alternative mode of politics in his analysis of 'middle opinion' in the thirties. In *Britain in the Age of Total War*, too, Marwick confirmed the First World War as the destroyer of the old world of imperialism and the Second World War as the creator of the new world of welfarism. The inter-war years were left ambivalently poised as a period of important and progressive social change tempered by drift and disaster in politics. Although his analysis of the period was nowhere near as dominated by high politics as that of Mowat, Marwick's shaping element in the transformation of Britain remained the emergence of new political ideas in the thirties, which only came to dominate during the Second World War.

A. J. P. Taylor contributed twice to the shaping of historical ideas on Britain's transformative journey through two world wars. In *English History, 1914–1945* (1965), Taylor presented his usual sardonic view of history as a series of events most of which no one either planned or foresaw, a series of accidents which left the high and the mighty tripped up, fumbling and perplexed. Neither did Taylor see much future in the liberal intelligentsia of the thirties, so loudly trumpeted by Mowat and Marwick. He found them just as muddled, confused and contradictory as the mainstream politicians, locating the moment of renewal in the Second World War itself, in the *ad hoc* response of government and people to short-term problems provided by the emergency. While both Mowat and Taylor saw the Second World War as a moment of rebirth, and both clearly saw the welfare age as redeeming the failure of the inter-war period, for Mowat that redemption was what the British people had been looking towards for twenty years; for Taylor it was just an accident: 'The British empire declined; the condition of the people improved. Few now sang "Land of Hope and Glory". Few even sang "England Arise". England had arisen all the same.'

Taylor's *Origins of the Second World War* (1961), though controversial chiefly for its treatment of German foreign policy in the

1930s, also sharpened criticism of British appeasement policy. Taylor argued that the appeasers simply handed Hitler on a plate opportunities which he had not expected, on the basis of a misguided code of international ethics. His comment, no doubt tongue-in-cheek, that 'Munich was a triumph for all that was best in the British way of life', prompted Hugh Trevor-Roper into a revealing misinterpretation, an irate response to the effect that Taylor might as well argue that the West should appease Soviet ambitions. Never was the function of history in reinforcing contemporary politics more abundantly clear. The critique of appeasement in the 1930s did indeed underlie much of the rhetoric of the Cold War, a belief that appeasement of the Soviets in the 1950s and 1960s would only produce an even more apocalyptic war than that against Hitler. The criticism of appeasement was founded on the notion that it is the prime responsibility of the state to prepare for the possibility of war, that might would only respect might, that appeasement had been a matter of national humiliation which had actually contributed to what it sought to avoid by encouraging aggression. To this, liberal-left historians added the implication that appeasement had been motivated by upper-class politicians who saw in Fascism a way of stopping communism. In *The Appeasers* (1967), by Martin Gilbert and Richard Gott, the 'Cliveden set' and the Anglo-German Fellowship were taken as evidence of a naïve conspiratorial group of crypto-Fascists at work in high places, who saw in Hitler's aggrandizement a way of saving their own privileged position.

The mainstream history of the years between the wars written in the post-war years both reflected and underpinned the politics of welfarism and of the Cold War, the mainstream politics of the post-war period. Written largely from a centre-left standpoint, this history posited the central role of the state as the engineer of national destiny. It was politicians, it was implied, who had failed Britain between the wars, and it was politicians who had engineered a new pact between nation and state in the war years. There was, however, a strand of writing about the inter-war period which suggested that the Mowat formula was not entirely stable, that it was in fact vulnerable. Among the New Left of the late 1960s and early 1970s, there were signs of growing unease with the cosy liberal consensus of the post-war years. Angus Calder's *The People's War* (1969) cast doubt on whether welfarism after the war had responded to the real victims of the inter-war years. For Calder, 1945 had seen a tepid reformism sitting on the radical ferment inherited from the inter-war years and sharpened in focus by the war. For New Left critiques of the inter-war period in the early 1970s, the real heroes and forces for change were not Mowat's liberal intelligentsia at all but, rather, the organized working class outside mainstream politics, celebrated by such as Margot Heinemann and Noreen Branson in *Britain in the 1930s* (1973). Heinemann's own personal history, dating back to deep political commitment as a young woman in the 1930s, took on a new perspective in the radicalized 1970s.

Recession to recovery and back to recession

The late 1960s and 1970s saw a marked decline in confidence in the post-war polity, and with that decline in confidence came marked changes in historical attitudes towards the period with which it had been so sharply contrasted. This happened not only among historians who were politically on the left, but also among historians of a more centrist approach. Economic historians who, anyway, have never been so inclined to the left as some of their colleagues in political and social history, began to look askance at the traditional picture of the inter-war years as one of unrelieved gloom. D. H. Aldcroft and H. W. Richardson, overviewing *The British Economy, 1870 to 1939* (1969), found that the 1930s had been a relatively prosperous period for Britain. The staple export industries had been in trouble, they argued, long before the First World War, whereas in the 1930s the development of the consumer economy had marked an overdue shift from the traditional and dangerous dependence on heavy industry. Aldcroft and Richardson had not discovered anything particularly new when they looked at the consumer economy, which had been recognized and commented upon by Mowat, Marwick and Taylor among others. What they were doing was seeing the significance of this development in a different light. While the widespread unemployment of these years had been the central feature for historians until this time, Aldcroft and Richardson put fuller emphasis on the rising living standards of the thirties, and argued that this should be seen as evidence of recovery, and the start of a new direction in the economy. While previously it had been seen as a damning indictment of the period that so many had been relatively prosperous while so many had been relatively poor, Aldcroft and Richardson suggested that the new prosperity should be seen in a much more positive light.

While there was controversy over whether what Aldcroft and Richardson were describing could be called a 'recovery', the effect was to switch historical attention from the failure of high politics and the problems of the unemployed, to the experience of the majority of people in the country. This majority was not unemployed, nor badly housed, nor suffering from malnutrition. Where the starkness of the contrast between the depressed areas and the rest of Britain had been used as an argument to show how unjust and unfair the inter-war years had been, the contrast was now being used to show how much progress there had been, even though there were unfortunate pockets of social distress left behind by the old economy. Sean Glynn and John Oxborrow attempted a judicious balance of the two views in their *Inter-War Britain: A Social and Economic History* (1976):

> popular versions stress the more pessimistic view, while emphasis on the record of economic growth is largely confined to academic works or textbooks. In this book we attempt to give weight to both aspects. No summary judgement of the period is possible. The inter-war years were a period which combined abnormally high unemployment with fairly rapid economic growth.

They also noted that there was significant development in areas such as housing standards, whereas in other areas of social policy there were clear failures. This was very much a transitional text in the history of the inter-war years. They noted the paradox and refused to judge. Publishers and students tend to prefer judgements rather than sitting on the fence, however, and signs of a major shift were not long in appearing.

In this period, Britain began to get used to large-scale unemployment again. By the mid-seventies, the number out of work was teetering on one million, a figure highly reminiscent of the inter-war years. In such economic circumstances, a new perspective developed. Suddenly, unemployment no longer seemed so alien from contemporary ideology. In 1977, Christopher Cook and John Stevenson synthesized and consolidated the new views of the period in *The Slump: Society and Politics during the Depression*. The title of the opening chapter told its own story: 'Myth and reality: Britain in the 1930s'. So, too, did the title of the second chapter: 'The dawn of affluence'. It was from the perspective that most people had prospered in the inter-war years that the authors proceeded to recontextualize the myths of 'the hungry thirties', the supposed challenge of the Communists, the blackshirts and the National Unemployed Workers' Movement. The threats from these quarters never materialized, Cook and Stevenson implied, because they were never more than the interest of a small minority in a nation better off than ever before. They ended with a chapter entitled 'The revolution that never was'. Their argument was that the 'dawn of affluence' made most people happy enough with the way things were in the depression, that even the worst-off gained from a relatively generous social policy and were not tempted, by and large, into extreme politics. The National Governments, so long the villains of the piece, emerged as the providers of a stable administration in a period of uncertainty, 'at once their greatest achievement and their greatest strength'. Labour, for all its lack of political success, had still managed to maintain the support of the vast bulk of the organized working class, 'a considerable feat', which stabilized the left in Britain just as the National Governments stabilized the right. The authors accepted that appeasement and unemployment were to leave a legacy of bitterness which helped to bring Labour to power in 1945 and spur the creation of the welfare state. Just as significant for the future, however, was the new affluence that had begun in the thirties and which, although temporarily interrupted by austerity in the post-war period, was to re-emerge to play just as important a transforming role in Britain as welfarism. The thirties, in other words, shaped the future not simply in negative but also in positive ways. Although post-war politics had been shaped by a rejection of the thirties, the affluence on which welfarism depended was actually a product of changes in the economy first emerging in the 1930s. Indeed, with the benefit of hindsight in the post-Thatcher years, we might even argue that continuing affluence was even more important than welfarism. Ultimately, after all, it was the threat to affluence that produced that politics of resentment which undercut the post-war political set-tlement and the whole ideology of welfarism.

The underlying suggestion in this line of argument is that, by and large, politics is not the engineer of national destiny at all. Long-term structural change in the national economy, as well as the impact of the global economy on the home country, are factors beyond the direct control of any single government. The test of government, rather, is whether it responds sensibly and maintains social and political consensus in periods of prolonged economic dislocation. On such a scale of measurement, politicians of the inter-war years seemed to score pretty well, certainly better than their successors in the 1960s and 1970s. Keith Middlemas's and John Barnes's portrait of *Baldwin* (1969) provided a much more sympathetic construction than that of G. M. Young in 1952. In the view of Middlemas and Barnes, Baldwin was a shrewd, pragmatic and comforting national leader who provided the Conservative party with the populist and progressive stance it needed to survive and prosper, rather than the devious, lazy and apathetic time-server he had seemed in the 1940s and 1950s. By 1977, even Ramsay MacDonald seemed ready for re-evaluation, as a man who created the Labour party in his own image and stuck to his principles, and a man who had been deserted by his party rather than vice versa. Perhaps this said as much about the predicament of the book's author, David Marquand, as right-wing Labour party member in the internecine warfare that was splitting the party in the late 1970s, as it did about MacDonald. At the time of writing, the greatest of the 'guilty men', Neville Chamberlain, still awaits his resurrectionist. But as governments in that period began to find it increasingly difficult to maintain their defence commitments, an increasingly sympathetic eye was turned on the problems faced by the appeasers. On the one hand, an American who worked on this period, R. P. Shay, still found it culpable that the Treasury should have exercised so much restraining control in *British Rearmament in the Thirties* (1977). On the other hand, from the vantage point of living in Britain on the verge of a new recession, George Peden found this perfectly understandable in *The Treasury and Rearmament* (1979). Appeasement began to lose its moral opprobrium as it came to be seen as perhaps the only rational policy for a nation in relative economic decline, with international commitments which were really too great for it any longer to bear. This was a point made most clearly, perhaps, by Paul Kennedy in the severely pragmatist stance of his *The Realities behind Diplomacy* (1985). More recently, however, there are signs of another change. R. A. C. Parker, in *Chamberlain and Appeasement* (1993), argues that for all the constraints imposed on government by the realities of the situation, Chamberlain failed to maintain the necessary united front against Germany, offered one-sided concessions and personalized his foreign policy, marginalizing the professionals. For Parker, it might be said, Chamberlain turned an already difficult situation into a desperate one which, if it did not actually produce the war, made it rather more difficult to fight than it might have been.

By the end of the 1970s, of course, the entire Beveridge–Keynes axis had come off the rails. The post-war consensus was dead, if it ever existed, and the New Right was in power. As the popular memory of the inter-war years and the war itself faded, new 'guilty men' were found among those who, it was now believed, had led Britain into the economic interventionist débâcle of the 1960s. In turn, New Right historians railed not against the politicians of the 1930s but at the supposed righting of the wrongs of the inter-war years in the post-war settlement. It is noticeable how far the centre of interest in contemporary British history has switched, over the last decade, from the inter-war period to the years after 1945. The attack on the post-war settlement, Correlli Barnett's *The Audit of War* (1986) being only the most virulent example, is a reflection of the way in which the agenda of contemporary politics has moved on. Other historians with a right-wing perspective, John Charmley for instance, have even felt nostalgic about Chamberlain because he had realized that the Empire would be lost if there were another war, and even dared to criticize Churchill for failing to realize that he would let Labour into power with a radical agenda.

A perspective from the end of the century

As the inter-war period has, with the passing of time, lost the immediate political resonances that it had from the 1940s through to the 1970s, so it has faded into what might be called 'proper' history, as distant from us as, say, 1910. The end of the Keynesian era in the late 1970s, and the switch of attack to the beginning of the age of welfare politics, the post-war settlement, has the result of leaving judgement on the inter-war period finely poised and, for that reason perhaps, fairly muted of late. The decline of interest in labour history has had an effect, too, since this period was one of the heroic ages of the sub-discipline. One subject that has continued to generate debate, however, is the culture of the period. It used to be fashionable to consider the 1930s as, among so many other epithets, 'the red decade'. Certainly there was a clear, if normally very temporary, shift to the far left among younger intellectuals and artists, which drew an inordinate amount of interest at the time and since. The 'Auden generation' managed an extraordinary degree of self-advertisement in their contempt for the 'old men' who ran the country. Cultural historians in the 1960s and 1970s, especially those with a literary background, perhaps gave them rather more attention than their numbers, or the extent of their commitment to the far left, actually warranted. In the long term, Marwick's 'middle way' among liberal intellectuals was to be more significant as evidence of ideological change in the élite than the temporary Marxism of a small group of poets. Just as important, however, has been an interest in the development of the culture of ordinary people, popular culture. For this was also the beginning of the age of the mass media, indeed of 'mass society'.

An interest in the history of cinema and in using cinema as a historical source goes back to the 1960s. This interest has very often concentrated on what was, after all, the classic age of cinema-going. Nicholas Pronay and Philip Taylor have focused on newsreel and documentary, in an attempt to explain how the new medium was used politically. The electorate had been vastly expanded in 1918, they point out, and cinema had great potential in organizing the views of the new voters. The Conservative party, they believe, was particularly adept in its use of cinema, especially in its wooing of the newsreel companies to give them access to a cinema audience of anything up to nineteen millions per week in the thirties. On a deeper level, film as entertainment can also provide real insight into the ideas of a time. What did people find entertaining at the time, and why? The way in which issues of gender, social class and national identity were negotiated for the mass audience has been treated by historians such as Jeffrey Richards in *The Age of the Dream Palace: Cinema and Society in Britain, 1930–1939* (1984) and Peter Stead's *Film and the Working Class* (1989), among others. This period was also the beginning of the age of radio, to which virtually all households had access by the outbreak of the Second World War, the significance of which has been treated by P. Scannell and D. Cardiff in the first volume of their *Social History of Broadcasting* (1991).

These developments have been involving historians not so much in a history of 'what happened' but, rather, a history of the sense people made of what was happening. The argument is not so much that people were simply brainwashed by propaganda, but that there was a subtle negotiation of current issues taking place in the mass media, even when what appeared to be on offer was 'simply entertainment', or even fantasy. The basic assumption of this kind of work is that it is important to take into account in the past not only the material world of work and politics, but also the ideological world of thoughts, of understanding. Indeed, it is only in the ideological world that the material world makes any kind of sense. Any credible explanation of the past must, therefore, take into account what people thought about what was happening to them, as much as what we, as historians in the present, think about what was happening to them.

Recently, the intervention of postmodernist thinking into the study of history has taken this argument a step further. The suggestion is that the gap between the past and the present is actually unbridgeable, that we will never get to 'what actually happened'; all that we have are 'representations' of the past, what people think happened. A particular example of this development in relation to our period is John Baxendale and Christopher Pawling, *Narrating the Thirties* (1996). The subtitle of the book is *A Decade in the Making: 1930 to the Present*. The authors argue, as the subtitle suggests, that understandings of the thirties have been constantly shifting, that there is not and has never been, one single and accurate reading of the thirties, or of any other period for that matter. The past is simply too complicated to be restored in any such way. The construction of the thirties at the time, by Mass Observation, by the Documentary Film Movement or by J. B. Priestley, has no more nor less weight than that of Mowat, Taylor or Stevenson and Cook. There is, in short, no access to the 'real' thirties at all, only ever-changing 'constructions' which reflect the particular concerns of groups both at the time and since.

What follows is to a large extent informed by views like these. It is not intended to be anything more nor less than a survey of the historiographical state of play. It is a view of the inter-war period which will hold good for the late twentieth century, but not for everybody, and perhaps not for long. As we have already seen, interpretations of the inter-war period have changed substantially since the beginning of the Second World War. The period has lost the immediate political burden it carried in the post-war world, so that interpretations may not change so rapidly in the future, but change they will, as indeed does interpretation of every period of the past. History, after all, is about the past, but it is made in the present. This particular story of what happened in Britain between the wars inevitably reflects the collapse of belief in what was seen to be the solution to pre-war problems just twenty or thirty years ago. In its backgrounding of politics, too, it reflects perhaps an end-of-millennium view that, in a democracy, politicians often get blamed (but just as often take the credit) for things over which they really have no control at all.

2. The Economy: The End of British Hegemony

For Britain, economics had been a relatively simple matter in the nineteenth century. Once the Corn Laws had been repealed in 1846 and protectionism abandoned, Gladstone had established free trade as the founding principle of Britain's economic policy and part of the great moral crusade for individual freedom. Chancellors of the Exchequer had simply applied the supposedly iron laws of supply and demand. With the whole world into which to expand, as the world's first industrial nation and with a strong mercantile tradition, Britain had grown and prospered seemingly effortlessly. From around the 1870s, however, there had been growing concern in the industrial and banking communities that the profits were not coming so easily, that the pace of industrial expansion was slowing down. Although these fears disappeared as trade recovered in the 1890s, many of the problems that had begun to show in the British economy in the last quarter of the nineteenth century were to resurface shortly after the First World War. The severity, and the longevity, of the depression that followed tested to destruction the notion that Britain could ever again restore her economic hegemony. In economic terms, Britain did relatively worse than other developed countries in the 1920s, such as the United States or France, but relatively better during the 1930s. Alongside this paradox was another, that while the depression hit some regions particularly hard, other areas did relatively well, particularly in the latter half of the period. Against the bleak images of the depressed areas must be set the new roads, the motor cars, the suburban housing estates, the domestic consumer durables, which suggest a well-off rather than a depressed society. Why was Britain doing relatively badly in the 1920s? How far was there a recovery in the 1930s with the development of a new consumer economy? Given the historiographical debate already noted about the role of the state and of politicians in framing what happened in Britain between the wars, we should also ask how far governments helped or hindered the processes at work.

Britain's self-image as a great power was at stake, but so were other things that were even more important. Responsible for the first time to a true mass electorate after 1918, governments were forced to consider whether the laws of *laissez-faire* were worth the candle. *Laissez-faire* had been part of the crusade for liberty, but economic failure was just as certainly a threat to liberty. Could a rate of at least 10 per cent unemployment be sustained indefinitely, or would Britain go the way of those states in central, southern and eastern Europe which were turning to totalitarian methods? Democracy itself appeared to be on the line. The reasons why Britain survived the depression with its institutions intact lie in a range of social, cultural and political factors covered in the chapters which follow. First, however, it is necessary to look at the scale of the economic problem the country faced. For economics lay at the root of all other problems.

The legacy of the nineteenth century

One particularly enticing explanation of the difficulties which Britain faced in the depression is that her long lead in world trade had allowed her to grow complacent. The 'early start' thesis contends that, although British industry and financial institutions were geared well enough to the easy trading conditions which applied while they were not in competition with other nations, they found it difficult to adapt to the circumstances that began to dominate in the last quarter of the nineteenth century, as the European and American industrialists moved into the world market. Britain's industrial revolution had been led by exports. During the 'great Victorian boom' of the mid-nineteenth century, the great staple export industries had come to predominate: coal, iron and steel, textiles and shipbuilding. From the 1870s, however, these industries appeared to be in the doldrums. Not only did Britain's reliance on exports make her particularly vulnerable to world recession, but the organization of these industries also made her vulnerable to competition. Traditionally, British industry revolved around the relatively small independent firm, in competition with other relatively small British firms for the world market. In the case of Germany and the United States, in particular, industrial organization had developed rather differently and allowed the emergence of huge corporate giants such as United States Steel or Krupp. British firms found it difficult to compete with the capitalization of these giants, and with the mass-production techniques that they inaugurated. Having tooled up for manufacturing techniques that were manpower-intensive, weaker British firms had to make up their minds whether they were able financially to scrap those techniques and invest in the new machinery that would make them competitive again. To do so, moreover, they would have to take on the established trade unions, dominated by those skilled men whose pay packets, as well as their social standing as the 'labour aristocracy', depended on keeping existing production techniques.

The staple export industries' domination of the British economy also had effects on other areas of the economy. The transport and building industries, for instance, were fundamentally reliant on what went on in heavy industry, so that any downturn in the staples' fortunes must have immediate blow-back effects on them as well. Financial institutions were also geared to the needs of the big exporters in the industrial economy, and seemed slow to see the need to invest in the 'secondary industrialization' – in the chemical and, later, electrical and other 'light industries' – which was soon to challenge heavy industry in terms of its share of world trade. Finance had itself become an important sector in the export economy, this time of capital. From early in the industrialization process, Britain had an inherent balance of payments problem and relied on invisible earnings, from foreign loans and insurance in particular, to fill the trade gap. This had made the City of London the capital of the money world, but the profits to be made in capital export were perhaps at the expense of the investment needs of industry.

During the 'great price fall' of the 1870s through to the 1890s, the first effects of international competition began to make themselves felt. These problems were disguised by imperial expansion in the 1880s and 1890s, by the armaments boom which began in the 1900s, and then by the unprecedented demand generated by the First World War. The coming of peace brought these long-standing structural problems back to the fore. While all developed countries would feel the impact of world recession, Britain would have had a set of structural problems to deal with even without the depression.

There had been only one sustained challenge to the dominant theory of free trade in this period, the tariff reform campaign. Joseph Chamberlain's response to the growing tendency of nations to defend their economies by a policy of tariffs on imports was to suggest throwing a tariff wall around the Empire. The result was a political catastrophe for the Conservative party, split asunder by

Chamberlain's campaign, and the reassertion of free-trade principles. By 1914, the economic worries of forty years before seemed a long way away, and liberal politicians believed that they could even fight a European war with a policy of 'business as usual'. With the benefit of hindsight, it is clear that such complacency was dangerous, but in 1914 few realized what the age of total war would entail.

Re-entering the peacetime economy

Even when it became clear that 'business as usual' would not win the war, it was easy to sustain the belief that this was only a temporary blip in the grand shape of things. During the First World War, military demand for whatever British industry could produce led to a collapse of *laissez-faire* principles. This collapse was only temporary, certainly, but it was massive while it lasted. The notion that the government which governed least was the government that governed best could not be sustained in total war. As a result, government undertook huge interventions in the organization of industry and of the labour force to sustain and increase production in conditions in which, of course, normal international trade could not operate. There was very little debate about whether controls would be abandoned when peace returned. The question, however, was how quickly normality could be restored. The sheer cost of paying for the war made the National Debt a pressing problem for any post-war government. Before the war the National Debt had stood at around £0.6 billion, but by 1919 it had risen to £7.7 billion, much of it contracted by borrowing at high rates of interest. The result was that debt service charges, let alone the cost of repaying the debt, rose from 11 per cent of government expenditure in 1913 to 20 per cent in 1920. A return to the economic principles that had given Britain prominence and financial stability for so long seemed the obvious, the clear-cut priority.

Given the unprecedented scale of the problem of the National Debt, it is at least understandable that sound finance and balanced budgets dominated Treasury thinking. Particularly important for the City of London was that the former primacy of sterling should be restored and that Britain should go back on to the Gold Standard. The Gold Standard, by which money supply was limited to the value of gold held in reserve, was abandoned during the war as Britain sold her overseas assets and the National Debt climbed. Thereafter, sterling had slowly but surely deteriorated against the neutral dollar. Pressure on public expenditure in the early 1920s to reduce the debt and force up the price of sterling had a deflationary effect on the economy. Trade seemed relatively buoyant, however, while German industry remained sapped by defeat and near-revolution. But, by 1921, Britain's international trade slumped; thereafter, there were to be never fewer than one million unemployed every year until 1940. The Lloyd George coalition and the Conservative administrations of Bonar Law and Baldwin which followed, continued the policy of abandoning the mesh of production, price and wage controls which had been necessary to run the war effort, opening industry to the full blast of competition. By 1925, moreover, the Chancellor of the Exchequer, Winston Churchill, had been convinced that the time was right to go back on to the Gold Standard at pre-war parity with the dollar. Such a move overpriced sterling by anything from 2.5 per cent (according to the Treasury) to 10 per cent (according to Keynes), automatically making British manufactured goods that much more expensive abroad.

The combined effect of the ending of wartime controls and the overpricing of sterling was difficult for industry in general. In the case of the coal industry it was potentially catastrophic. The coal industry was typical of the British industrial structure of the nineteenth century. In the early 1920s, it still consisted of nearly 1,500 firms, some of which were only marginally viable financially, either because of the quality of their coal or because of geological conditions. All of them had been shielded from competition during the war, when coal prices and wages had been guaranteed and the mines had been nationalized in all but name. In 1921, the industry was decontrolled by government. The owners responded by announcing a cut in wages, the only way they felt they could deal with the adjustment necessary to cope with the end of the subsidy. A general strike was only avoided by the failure of the transport workers to support the mineworkers. A year later, in response to the overpricing of sterling with the return to the Gold Standard, the owners announced another cut in wages. This time the TUC responded, though the General Strike fizzled out in inter-union recrimination in nine days in May 1926. The implications of the General Strike, however, were far more wide-ranging than its immediate outcome, for the events in the coal industry raised many questions about the political and social consequences of sticking rigidly to *laissez-faire* principles. Government had refused to intervene in negotiations between owners and miners because, they said, it was not their concern. The miners' case was that the situation in the mining industry had been caused by government, by its policies of decontrol and deflation. If the future of the mining industry lay with its rationalization and reorganization, moreover, then it was unrealistic to expect the mine owners to do it themselves; it was a task which only government intervention could undertake. In the meantime, the spectre of the General Strike prompted those on both the moderate right and the moderate left to seek more accommodating policies. In the Mond–Turner talks of the late 1920s, both sides of industry sat down to try to agree ways of avoiding the confrontations that recession inevitably produced. Widespread industrial warfare was probably avoided in this period in spite of, rather than because of, government economic policy.

Working with a deflationary financial policy, with sterling over-priced, with poorly organized export industries still specializing in areas of production coming to be regarded as outmoded, Britain was badly positioned at the beginning of the slump. It is important to remember, however, that Britain's economic problems were rooted in her industrial past. Financial policy in the 1920s did not help matters, but it does not appear to have been the root cause of the problem. Between 1899 and 1937, Britain lost 10.1 per cent of her share of world trade. While only 17 per cent of the manufacturing output of the United States (the most successful exporter of the period) was in the sector in which Britain had traditionally excelled, 42 per cent of Britain's output remained in this category. But it is also clear that Britain was not competing well even within the traditional sector. Japan, for example, also had her exports con-centrated in the traditional sector yet still managed to increase her share of world trade by 6 per cent over the period. Textile production was at the front of Japanese exports: this was especially ominous, since Britain had relied on exports to sell 80 per cent of her own textile production. In the relatively rich and expanding markets of Europe and North America, moreover, Britain was doing particularly badly, her exports to Europe actually falling by 20 per cent between 1913 and 1929. Neither could Britain rely indefinitely on the underdeveloped world. The primary producing nations were suffering from adverse terms of trade in the 1920s, which encouraged them to rely on home production for goods they could not afford to buy from abroad. India, for example, increased her cotton goods output fourfold in the inter-war years, while British textile sales to the subcontinent dropped to just one-tenth of their former level.

Britain performed relatively poorly in the 1920s primarily because she had come to specialize (and ineffectively at that) in exporting low-income products to low-income countries, rather than high-income products to high-income countries. While in the United States in the 1920s, there was large-scale investment in areas such as motor car manufacture and the electrical industry, this was markedly less true of Britain. As we shall see, these new industries did not necessarily make for stability in the long term, but they did provide new growth. In Britain, the new industries, which were to become more significant in the next decade, were as yet too small to make a real impression on an economy dominated by industries whose products large parts of the world either did not want or could not afford to buy. To put Britain's economic performance in perspective, however, it should be pointed out that she was doing no worse in the 1920s than she had done previously. Indices of industrial production show that British industrial output was growing on average by 2.8 per cent per annum during the 1920s, about the same as it had done in most periods since 1860 (table 1), though there had been artificially high levels of production during the First World War, of course. The problem with the economy in the 1920s was that Britain was not doing as well as her competitors, and was consequently losing her share of the world market.

The 1931 crisis and new directions in policy

If Britain's problems were not caused primarily by financial policy in the 1920s, the crisis of world finance that began on Wall Street in 1929 was to have a profound effect on the British economy in the 1930s. The return to the Gold Standard in 1925, at pre-war parity with the dollar, was intended to restore the sterling supremacy of the nineteenth century. In fact, the First World War and the 1920s had seen the inexorable rise to global power of the American economy and the dollar. The crushing impact of the Wall Street crash, not only on Britain but on every other nation except the Soviet Union, showed just how much power relationships in the world had changed since 1914. The United States had, in effect, financed much of the war efforts of the victorious combatants between 1914 and 1918. The decision taken at Versailles in 1919 to impose reparations payments on Germany, as a punishment for having supposedly caused the war, allowed America's debtors to repay some of that debt. Of the $2 billion collected from Germany between 1924 and 1929, $1 billion was passed on from Europe to the USA as interest and debt repayment. In turn, the USA loaned major sums to countries in central and eastern Europe, especially Germany, to finance their balance of payments deficits. With the benefit of hindsight, this recycling of money by American lenders was, at best, reckless, though it should be said that contemporaries consistently overestimated German growth rates and her financial solvency. It is now clear that Germany was simply unable to sustain the burden of external debts in the 1920s. Gigantic speculation in US bonds led to a spectacular collapse in 1929, after which Americans began calling in their debts.

During 1930 and 1931 a wave of bank failures spread across the United States and Europe. In the absence of accommodation from their creditors, primary producing countries, including Australia, New Zealand, Canada and a raft of Latin American countries, were forced to abandon the Gold Standard and devalue their currencies. Britain's own position as a creditor nation was too weak to stand the strain, particularly after the collapse of the German banking system in the summer of 1931. Determined to maintain the Gold Standard, as the Conservatives had been before them, the Labour government watched helplessly as £350 million of foreign money left the country. The Bank of England, even with a hike in interest rates, could not survive that sort of pressure for long without depleting its gold reserves entirely or negotiating foreign loans. The latter was bound to be difficult to attain in the international financial context, unless Britain looked financially solvent. Confidence waned as the budget surplus, £100 million in 1928, turned into a budgetary deficit of roughly the same size in 1931. Then the report of the May Committee in August 1931 forecast a budget deficit of £120 million for 1932, and a deficit of £150 million on the Unemployment Insurance Fund. The run on gold turned into a rout. Already politically weak as a minority government, MacDonald's Cabinet collapsed in trying to agree the public expenditure cuts deemed essential to restore the confidence necessary to secure foreign loans. A coalition, led by MacDonald but entirely dependent on the Conservatives, won the ensuing election on a 'doctor's mandate' to do what was necessary to save gold. Yet even the ensuing emergency budget of cuts in public expenditure could not stop the flow of gold from London and, within a month of being elected to save it, the National Government rushed through legislation to take Britain off the Gold Standard.

Once the country was freed from the strict financial straitjacket imposed by the Gold Standard, the way was at least open to end the deflationary policies of the 1920s and to look for industrial recovery. Britain had seized an advantage by deflating relatively early, but most other countries also left gold in the next few years, including the USA in 1933. Britain's advantage was thus soon whittled away. In the period of world-wide loss of confidence that followed the crash, moreover, many countries were tempted into self-preserving policies, imposing tariffs and import quotas which did not make international trading conditions any easier. Britain herself imposed tariffs with imperial preference, a tax on imports with concessionary rates for countries in the British Empire, as the severity of the depression finally undermined the ideological commitment to free trade which had ruled for so long. A tariff of 10 per cent was introduced in 1932, effectively raised to 20 per cent thereafter in the case of most manufactured goods, even higher in the case of iron and steel imports. Such protective measures may well have done something to shield British producers for the domestic market, but they did not stop the increasing economic penetration of Britain, as the Americans began to invest directly in British firms or to open up satellites in Britain, as in the case of AEI, Remington Rand and Hoover. Since Britain relied so heavily on exports, anyway, it was not clear that Britain would gain as much from protecting her domestic market as she would lose from other countries protecting theirs. In the complete antithesis of free trade, Britain then began to use the tariff as a threat to wring concessions from the dominions, as at the Ottawa Conference in 1932, and then in a series of bilateral trade agreements with Argentina, Scandinavia and the Soviet Union.

After a brief flirtation with high interest rates in the wake of the 1931 crisis, to restore confidence in sterling, the 1930s as a whole was a period of cheap money. Low interest rates made the government's international debts cheaper to repay. They also made it cheaper for businesses to invest, and thus encouraged growth. Industry, however, seems not to have taken too great an advantage. The number of bank loans to industry, both heavy and light, actually fell: the only substantial rise in the number of advances was to the building trades, but there was a rise in private loans and overdrafts. This would suggest that, if cheap money did not encourage industrialists to borrow, it did encourage private citizens to consume.

This was perhaps more clear in relation to the building industry than in any other sector. For the average home-buyer in the 1930s, the cost of mortgage repayments fell by a quarter, and the demand for new housing was to be one of the clearest signs of an economic recovery that occurred in the decade (table 2). Government's contribution to this was to restrict public-sector borrowing, which meant balancing the budget.

Governments in Sweden, Germany, France and the United States deliberately incurred budgetary deficits to promote economic growth. Britain, on the other hand, stayed loyal to the principle of aiming to balance the budget until she was forced to abandon it with the pressure for rearmament. Arguments about the advisability of British fiscal policy in the 1930s have changed with the intellectual climate. Keynesians found it easy to criticize the refusal of government to consider a deliberately reflationary policy. It must be remembered, however, that it was only in 1936 that Keynes himself put together the intellectual apparatus that underpinned the practice of counter-cyclical investment. There was no 'Keynesian alternative' as such before the publication of the General Theory although admittedly there were the practical examples of what other countries were doing to imitate. When the government did resort to borrowing to pay for rearmament, Keynes actually agreed with the Treasury that the ceiling put on borrowing was essential if inflation was to be avoided. Keynes never really advocated the huge rises in public-sector borrowing that were incurred in his name in the 1960s and 1970s. It is highly unlikely anyway that Keynesian methods, on their own, could have cured the British problem. At any rate, they would have been enormously expensive if they were to make any impression. Estimates by economic historians reckon that an outlay of £750 million would have been required to deal with the three million unemployed of 1932, which would have virtually doubled the budget outlay in that year and would have amounted to over 19 per cent of the entire Gross National Product. Although Keynesian methods may secure near-full employment in an economy which is working somewhere near efficiency, they were not meant to reflate a globally burst balloon. What the National Governments offered instead was political stability and 'sound finance', on the grounds that restoration of confidence both at home and abroad was government's real contribution to recovery.

Government was prepared to make some moves in the direction of helping industry to rationalize, to reorganize to meet world competition more efficiently. For a generation of historians used to state intervention on the scale that became normal after 1945, this action was too little and too late, but it did show that government became aware that there was a problem which, perhaps, only the state could solve. The British Shipping Act of 1935 provided a modest public subsidy for a scheme to build new ships, on condition that competition between British shippers was reduced and freight rates were increased. Substantial loans were made available to railway companies to modernize, and Imperial Airways was virtually held aloft by subsidies. In these moves, the infrastructure of transport was at least pointed in the right direction. The attempt to reorganize the coal industry under the Coal Mines Act of 1930 proved less satisfactory, largely through the opposition of mine owners. The British Iron and Steel Federation was set up in 1934 to foster reorganization of the heavy-metals industries, which secured tariff protection in return. The Cotton Industry Act of 1936 set up a board to buy and scrap spare capacity in textile manufacturing. These measures may have gone a little way to reduce internal competition and to allow the industries to face up to the realities of international trading in the 1930s. Their weakness was that they still relied on the co-operation of the industries themselves. Their relative failure prepared the ground for the much larger interventions that occurred in the Second World War and in the nationalization programme of the Labour government of 1945.

It cannot be said that the changes in policy direction that occurred after the sterling crisis of 1931 were innovative in a major way. Nevertheless, the alarming international situation of the late 1930s pushed government into spending on rearmament which it would rather not have incurred, spending which undoubtedly did contribute to a boom in the last years of peace. Government was also prepared to experiment, as was shown in tariff policy and in attempts at industrial reorganization, measures which would have been wholly unthinkable twenty-five years before. On the whole, however, government hoped to secure recovery by not being radical, by inspiring confidence rather than excitement.

'Recovery' in the 1930s

If a recovery occurred in the 1930s, it was not directed by government policy, though at least government policy did nothing to hinder it. Signs of recovery in the decade centre on consumer spending, on a new 'development block' within the economy. Revisionist economic historians argue that the depression in Britain proved to be, in a sense, self-righting. Prices fell and remained low through most of the inter-war period, but wages and salaries did not fall as fast, with the result that real incomes rose substantially, by as much as 24 per cent over the whole period and by 19 per cent in the 1930s (tables 3, 4, 5). Although worries about unemployment may have restricted spending through much of the period, returning confidence in the 1930s fed this increase in real incomes into consumer spending – on housing, cars and other consumer durables – which in turn dragged up the rest of the economy.

There were certainly rises in employment in the building trade and in the service industries. Car manufacture more than doubled in the 1930s. Three million new houses were built in the decade, increasing by nearly one-third the total available housing stock, most of these in the private sector (table 2). There are problems, however, with describing this as a 'recovery'. First, these developments affected only certain regions, notably the south-east and the Midlands, and hardly impacted at all on the depressed areas where the staple export industries were located. There is little evidence that the consumer boom dragged the older industries into recovery. The consumer boom demanded steel, certainly, but looked to new power sources, to electricity rather than directly to coal, for instance. Second, the older industries, though they declined in size, were still larger than the new industries in terms of their total output. They were also more efficient, in terms of productivity per worker. In other words, however fast the new industries may have been growing in the second half of the inter-war period, they were not yet leading the economy in any meaningful way. Third, the consumer industries tended to be remarkably thirsty for imports of raw materials, and no more successful than the older industries in securing export markets. This was hardly helpful for the future of the balance of payments. Fourth, the consumer economy was inherently unstable. Consumer durables are bought by households, not large companies with large financial reserves, and households are notoriously sensitive to cyclical fluctuations. In fact, in the case of the United States, it has been argued that the development of consumerism actually helped to cause the depression, since even a small decrease in household income, or a small increase in the threat of job losses, could have quite disproportionate effects on confidence and thus on trading.

Perhaps consumerism would best be described as a new development in the economy, rather than a recovery, bringing with it more and different problems without solving the problem of the decline of the staple exporters.

The fact remains that the industries and the work-force on which Britain's economic greatness had depended had gone into what appeared to be an irreversible decline. Although the Second World War was to have a similar effect to the First World War in stimulating demand for everything these industries could produce, only nationalization could save them. Although the Conservatives initially opposed this, by the 1960s even they had accepted what seemed to be the new inevitable facts of life. In the post-Keynesian era, it is fashionable to criticize the state interventions of the post-Second World War period, just as it was fashionable in the 1950s and 1960s to criticize the inter-war period for a lack of state intervention. The point should be made that there was no clear alternative on offer in the 1920s and 1930s. The Labour party was even more Gladstonian in its economic policy than the Conservatives, who were at least ready to countenance the end of free trade, a move described at the time as 'lunatic' by Labour's Clement Attlee. Neither is it clear that a programme of massive government investment would have solved the problem of unemployment without first breaking the back of the economy. Unlike the governments of the 1960s and 1970s, governments in the inter-war years did not have an International Monetary Fund to which they could run. There appeared to be no alternative to financial orthodoxy. Neither is it clear that post-war governments fared any better: Britain's relative economic decline has continued, after all, with or without state intervention.

In the 1930s, the British economy was evolving into its recognizably modern form, dependent no longer on heavy industry but, increasingly, on a volatile consumer market, which left some areas of the nation relatively impoverished. Virtually everyone got richer in the depression, though some got richer than others. Government, except in minor ways, neither helped nor hindered this process. The firmest conclusion would be that government made things slightly worse than they need have been in the 1920s, and slightly better than they might have been in the 1930s. But the export industries would have been put under intense pressure in the 1920s with or without deflationary fiscal policy, and the consumer boom would have happened in the 1930s with or without cheap money or rearmament.

3.   Society and Government

During the depression most of the British were getting richer. Contemporaries may not have noticed this fact, because money wages and salaries were not increasing, but what those wages and salaries were buying was certainly increasing (tables 3, 4). Falling prices meant a rise in real wages and salaries of about one-quarter. Since families were also getting smaller, as knowledge of birth control measures spread into the working class, families had fewer mouths to feed. Food itself declined markedly as a percentage of family expenditure, even though people were eating substantially more, as food prices declined. Of course there was poverty, but not much of it was of the primary and widespread kind that had scarred Britain in the nineteenth century. Indeed, the very definition of poverty changed to reflect the changed social expectations that came with the general rise in living standards. In the 1890s, social investigators had defined poverty at what we would now term subsistence level, the level below which physical deterioration set in. By the 1930s, Seebohm Rowntree, in his second social survey of York, felt that a little money for alcohol, cigarettes, radio, newspapers and a few other items should be included in the basic requirements for life in a civilized society. [**DOCUMENT III**] The fact that poverty persisted, however, was even more striking because the country as a whole was so much better off. Unemployment was only part of the problem. Inadequate wages of some of those in work continued to be a problem in some areas. Childhood and parenthood still tended to be difficult times financially, even though family sizes were declining. Poverty in old age remained a scar on social life as life expectancy increased. [**DOCUMENT IV**] Striking, too, was the pattern of regional variation in poverty. The areas that produced so much wealth in the nineteenth century were now impoverished, while the south, with the exception of London virtually a depressed area for over a century, emerged as the new centre of economic opportunity.

It is clear that the social reforms of the pre-1914 Liberal governments had done much to offset some of the major causes of poverty. Seebohm Rowntree paid tribute to the development of the social services, and to public intervention both at national and local level on matters such as sanitation and housing, in improving both the quality and the length of life in the years since he had produced his first report in 1899. The introduction of unemployment benefits and health insurance were major steps in combating two of the most obvious causes of poverty, and old age pensions kept at least some aged people out of the workhouse. There was much, however, still to be done. During the inter-war years, as the depression ground on, governments struggled hard to come to terms with the social consequences. Such measures, however, had to be constricted by what was considered financially possible.

The changing pattern of the population

The population of England, Scotland and Wales in 1911 was 40.8 million. By 1921, it had risen to 42.7 million, and to 44.8 million by 1931. Unfortunately, the census that should have been taken in 1941 was cancelled because of the war. By 1951, the population had grown to 48.8 million but, since we know that there was a baby boom in the late 1940s, much of the growth that took place between 1931 and 1951 may have been in the last few years of that period. Although the population continued to rise, then, it was growing at a much slower rate than previously. This may well have reflected the growing understanding of methods of birth control. The average couple typically had three children before the First World War, only 2.1 in the inter-war period. There was also a marked shift in the pattern of the labour force. Manual workers accounted for about 75 per cent of the total labour force in 1911, 70 per cent in 1931, and less than 65 per cent by 1951. This was the effect of the relative decline of heavy industry, with its traditional emphasis on manual labour. The rise of the service and consumer sectors of the economy, with their emphases on the skills associated with white-collar workers, was reflected in the growth of the lower middle class. This section of society grew from about 19 per cent of the labour force in 1911, to 23 per cent in 1931, and to over 30 per cent in 1951. Since we know that working-class families tended to be bigger than middle-class ones, and since manual labour still declined proportionately, there must have been some considerable social migration to the lower middle class by the children of manual-labouring parents during our period. Independent employers, meanwhile, remained stable at under 7 per cent of the occupied population.

The changing shape of the economy, and the new employment pattern, were also reflected in regional variations in the population. The biggest rise in the population between the wars occurred in London and the south-east, some 18 per cent. But it was the population of outer London which increased the most, as the development of suburbia ate into available space in the Home Counties and produced the modern commuter-land. While the population of the Midlands, also relatively prosperous between the wars, increased by 11 per cent, Lancashire did not grow at all, the population of the north-east and central Scotland fell a little while that of south Wales fell by nearly 10 per cent. The age structure of the regions where population was either stable or actually falling suggests that there was a great deal of migration to more prosperous areas by younger people, leaving behind an ageing population which was in turn likely to contribute to a vicious downward spiral of economic opportunity in the region.

While the rate of population growth was slowing down and families were becoming smaller, people were living longer. Life expectancy for a boy born in the decade before the First World War was 51.5 years, for a girl 55.4 years; by the 1930s the figures were 58.7 and 62.9 respectively. Even so, it was to be another thirty years before one could reasonably hope to live the biblical span of 'three score years and ten'. Over the same period, the infant mortality rate fell notably, from 105 per 1,000 live births before the war to 60 in 1930. Once again, the national figures are perhaps less important than the social and regional differences that they mask. The Home Counties had a death rate 20 per cent below the national average, while that for Jarrow was 30 per cent higher. Partly, this was due to the different age structures of the prosperous and the depressed areas, but it was a fact that a child born into the professional middle class, then as now, simply had a much greater chance of living beyond the average life expectancy than did the child of a manual labourer.

Unemployment

The decline in heavy industry produced unemployment not simply because lack of trade meant that fewer workpeople were needed, but also because these industries deliberately shed labour and increased productivity per worker, to make themselves more competitive. Thus, the number of coal-miners fell from over one million in 1920 to 675,000 by 1939, while the iron and steel industry reduced its work-force from over 500,000 to under 350,000. At the same time, there were new job opportunities in the consumer industries and in the development of the public services, notably in electricity. There were problems in matching the new jobs with the jobless, however. First, the new jobs tended not to be in areas where there was high unemployment and, second, patriarchal attitudes dubbed many of the new jobs 'women's work'. The first of these problems could only be solved by migration, which was difficult for those older unemployed with many family and other ties. The government's Industrial Transference Scheme was designed to help this migration but it proved a singularly unattractive form of resettlement. The effect of migration, moreover, was simply to consolidate the problems of the older population left behind. The second 'problem' meant that there was something of a small boom in female employment. While the war caused a spectacular rise in female employment in munitions and in engineering, these jobs were for the duration of the war only. Still, the number of women in employment rose from 5.2 million in 1911 to 6.3 million in 1931. Admittedly, this rise is roughly in line with the rise in the number of women of working age in the population. It does seem to show, on the other hand, that women did not suffer disproportionately from unemployment, though that was small comfort, given the range of social disadvantages to be catalogued later. For working people as a whole, unemployment changed from an annual average of 4.8 per cent in the two decades before 1914 to an annual average of never less than 10 per cent between 1920 and 1940, reaching as high as 22 per cent in 1932. The mean for the period 1920 to 1940 was 14 per cent (table 6).

Most unemployment, it must be stressed, was short-term. Par-ticularly during the 1920s, it was unusual for people to be out of work for more than six months though, of course, they might be made unemployed more than once. In the 1930s, however, there emerged the particular problem of the long-term unemployed, notably in the heavy-industry areas, many miles from the new job opportunities. By mid-1932 the long-term unemployed amounted to over 16 per cent of the unemployed. As employment recovered later in the 1930s, moreover, the long-term unemployed increased as a proportion of the smaller total, highlighting the plight of what came to be known as the distressed areas which the new economy was simply leaving behind. Long-term unemployment was a particular problem in towns which had relied on one industry to provide virtually all employment, towns like Jarrow in County Durham, for instance, entirely reliant on ship-building, or the Rhondda, entirely reliant on coal. [**DOCUMENT V**] Northern England and south Wales contained less than 50 per cent of the insured work-force but, in 1935, accounted for more than 70 per cent of unemployment. Average unemployment between 1929 and 1936 was 16.9 per cent for the country as a whole; in the south-east it was 7.8 per cent, in the north-east it was 22.7 per cent, in Scotland 21.8 per cent, in Wales an appalling 30.1 per cent

Employment insurance before 1914 had covered only a small part of the total work-force, and guaranteed benefit only for the short period before, it was assumed, the trade cycle would turn. Given that most unemployment lasted less than six months, the extension of unemployment benefit to virtually all of the work-force during the inter-war period covered most people's basic needs most of the time. This is not to imply that unemployment was in any sense pleasurable. Benefits were, on the other hand, more generous than in most other countries, and generally given on less stringent terms. Benefits were also related to the size of families, whereas wages were not. Consequently, although for most people unemployment meant a drastic reduction in income, many found themselves better off on the dole than at work. Attempts to square this circle by keeping unemployment benefits lower than low wages did, of course, rebound on families with young children. [**DOCUMENT X**] In York, for example, Rowntree found that the inadequate wages of those in work with large families were as big a cause of poverty as unemployment. In fact, unemployment would have been a better option, financially, for many of them.

Problems did occur, however, where people had to live for more than six months on this income. Even greater problems occurred when the state found the level of expenditure on unemployment intolerable and decided to reduce it, as in the wake of the May Committee report in 1931. The wives of the unemployed men found themselves constantly cutting back on their own diets, clothing and medical needs in order to keep the men in the family 'ready for work'. In the wake of the 1931 cut of 10 per cent in benefits, however, not even they could cope. The Save the Children Fund reported a noticeable rise in malnutrition between 1931 and 1932.

The decision to implement the Family Means Test on benefits, also taken in response to the financial emergency, played havoc with the patriarchal culture of unemployed coalminers and steelworkers, unable to resign themselves to the idea of living off the income of their working wives or their working children. A major bone of contention was the system of administration of unemployment relief which, for much of the inter-war period, allowed widely differing rates of relief to be paid out in different parts of the country. Unemployment insurance was actually only one part of the system of relief; there was also the old Poor Law, or Public Assistance as it became known after 1928, for those who had used up their statutory entitlement to insurance benefit. There was also Transitional Benefit, which had been introduced in 1921 as a short-term measure to deal with long-term unemployment but soon became institutionalized. Public Assistance and Transitional Benefit were administered locally, which gave the opportunity for some local Public Assistance Commissions, especially those that were Labour-controlled, to give out more generous benefits than the government guidelines allowed.

The Board of Guardians Default Act of 1926 gave government the power to replace local guardians if they consistently ignored government norms. In the wake of the 1931 cuts, however, a substantial number of local administrations simply refused to implement the means test. In 1934, government responded with an Unemployment Act which set up Unemployment Assistance boards, controlling all three types of pay-out, and standardizing rates nationally. The aim of the scheme was, of course, to economize, but its true significance was somewhat deeper. Effectively, this Act was the decisive break from the Poor Law tradition that social distress was a problem for the locality. From now on, it was firmly a national responsibility, and nationally administered. This was no paradigm shift, however, for in other areas of social policy, central government continued to rely on local government to administer local needs. Nevertheless, it was an important breach in traditional principle.

Government also abandoned tradition in measures taken to deal with the depressed areas, in order to kick-start them back to life. Rather than rely entirely on the Industrial Transference Scheme, government introduced the Special Areas Act in 1934, which put unpaid commissioners in the areas to attempt to attract new investment. The funding of the scheme was paltry, but in 1937 the Special Areas Amendment Act proved a more serious attempt at social engineering. This gave remissions in rent, rate and taxes to firms moving into municipally run industrial estates. By the end of the 1930s, the Barlow Commission on the Distribution of the Industrial Population was looking at some very far-reaching proposals, involving the redevelopment of congested and distressed areas and the dispersal of industry on a national scale. This was to be the blueprint for the New Towns policy of post-1945. Overall, it could be said that the piecemeal extension of unemployment benefit to virtually all the employed population, in spite of the cuts and the means test, did allow most of the unemployed at least to get by. In the Special Areas Amendment Act, moreover, and in the working of the Barlow Commission, it is possible to see the germ of an idea that was to reach fruition after the Second World War: that the state had not just the right but the duty to provide the opportunities for jobs, even if it involved interfering with the supposedly iron laws of the free market.

Housing

For the large majority of people in inter-war Britain, unemployment was a risk rather than a reality. Nowhere is the revolution in rising expectations which characterized most people's lives more apparent than in the building boom. Anyone transported from the south-east in 1911 to the south-east in 1939 would have been astonished by the improvements in housing, by the development of huge, low-density housing estates, by the electric lighting, the vacuum cleaners, the indoor bathrooms and lavatories, the gardens, the cars in the garages. Anyone making the same time-journey in Liverpool or Glasgow would have been less astonished, though the change was still remarkable. By the outbreak of the Second World War, one-third of all families in Britain were living in houses which had been built since 1918, and built to standards which were wholly different from those that had been typical of the nineteenth century. Well over four million houses were built in Britain between the wars (table 2). About half of these were built by private enterprise, and the rise in owner-occupation was the most obvious sign of the rise in real incomes in the period. The building society was an increasingly popular way of saving and borrowing money for private individuals between the wars, and cheap-money policy in the 1930s made house-buying a particularly attractive investment. Builders were also able to put together complete packages, with laid-out gardens and household electrical goods, at bargain prices. Owner-occupiers amounted to 10 per cent of all families in Britain in 1911, but 31 per cent by the end of the 1930s.

There was just as significant a change in municipally provided housing. Lloyd George became infamous for his unfulfilled promise to the First World War soldiers that there would be homes fit for heroes to live in when they returned from the trenches. Addison's Housing Act of 1919, which required local authorities to make good their housing deficiencies and provided central government subsidies, fell victim to the cuts in public expenditure in 1921. The incoming Conservatives reintroduced the subsidy in 1923, however, and, in spite of continuous budgetary pressure on housing subsidies, further legislation in 1924 and 1930 by Labour, and by the Coalition in 1933 and 1935, showed the commitment of government to modernize the housing stock. Although the legislation, particularly that of 1923, did encourage private building as well as public, it was generally designed to provide council houses and flats. Before the First World War, council-house tenancy made virtually no statistical impact, but by the end of the inter-war period 14 per cent of all families lived in council accommodation.

Inevitably, such an improvement in housing standards brought complaints from those who had to put up with what had now become substandard accommodation. A total of 350,000 properties were demolished, but it was reckoned that there were still over 600,000 houses that could be classed as slums at the end of the period. [DOCUMENT VI] Many of these were to be demolished, though in a rather haphazard fashion, by the Luftwaffe in 1940 and 1941, creating a new housing problem for the post-war years. In the meantime, overcrowding remained a problem in many poorer areas. This was probably not because of a shortage of decent housing as such but because overcrowding was the only way of making the rent affordable. [DOCUMENT VII] In fact, there were some 360,000 properties unoccupied during the 1930s. For the worst-off section of society, even a council house was still beyond their means. Only about 4 per cent of the private new houses in York were occupied by families which Rowntree would define as skilled working-class, whereas skilled workers and clerks dominated the council estates. Government subsidies did not, as yet, make it possible for all but a small number of local authorities to offer rent reductions to those at the bottom of the social scale. In 1935, when overcrowding was reckoned as more than three people living in two rooms, the total of overcrowded houses in Britain was 350,000. To put that apparently large figure into perspective, however, it amounted only to three or four per cent of the total housing stock.

As in the case of unemployment, the plight of the badly housed may be seen as a major problem not because it was typical, but because it was very atypical. In a period when living standards were improving so rapidly, it was perhaps inevitable that some sections of society would be left behind, that what had been considered virtually normal living for the last half-century would, within twenty years, become a 'social problem'. Coincidentally, the problems of over-crowded slum living happened to occur most commonly in the depressed areas, because high-density housing had been the quickest and most simple way of accommodating the rapidly growing work-force in those areas in the nineteenth century. Government had contributed, and probably substantially, to the improvement in housing conditions: directly, through subsidies, even if these were not adequate to deal with the entire problem, and indirectly, by keeping interest rates low, which encouraged cheap mortgages. Ultimately, however, the real root of the improvement in housing was the fact that anyone who remained employed between the wars had a lot more money to spend.

Health

One rather gloomy indication of the general improvement of the standard of living in Britain in the inter-war years was the decline in deaths from scarlet fever, tuberculosis and infectious diseases, and the rise in deaths from cancer and heart disease, the killers of affluent rather than poor societies. Undoubtedly, the decline in infectious disease was accomplished by the series of public-health acts which had begun in the nineteenth century and which continued between the wars. These aimed at improving the water supply, improving sanitation and, as we have seen, improving the quality of housing. Medical opinion was less convinced in the inter-war period, however, that environment was the be-all and end-all of good health. A study of what happened when half the population of a slum area in Stockton-on-Tees was moved to a new estate found that those who had moved to a better environment actually suffered a worse death rate than those who remained behind. The study concluded that the higher rents on the new estate had prompted people to cut back on their diet. A better environment might lessen the risk of infection, but nutrition was the key to fighting infection. While people were eating more than ever before in the inter-war years, as food prices went down, they still had to be educated in the importance of vitamins, minerals and a generally balanced diet. While one did not have to be poor to lack education in dietetics, it tended to be the case that nutritionally significant foods like fresh vegetables, fish and fruit were more expensive than potentially damaging foods, and were the first to go when money became tight.

Healthy physiques remained the privilege of the better-off. Although all children were taller and heavier in York in the 1930s than in the 1890s, the better-off children were substantially taller and heavier than the impoverished. Rowntree's and similar studies seemed to suggest that, though very few might now die of starvation in Britain, the long-term effects of malnutrition in childhood could be very damaging in terms of life expectancy. Malnutrition probably contributed substantially to keeping maternal mortality at a worryingly high level as well, as impoverished mothers-to-be denied themselves those expensive foods which were so important to a healthy pregnancy. If expectant mothers had themselves suffered from malnutrition during childhood, moreover, it seemed to heighten the risk that they had developed some pelvic or other irregularity that made pregnancy more dangerous. The research of Sir John Boyd Orr, published as *Food, Health and Income* in 1936, suggested that only half of the population of the country, the better-off half, was eating a diet adequate for sustained good health. [DOCUMENT VIII] Needless to say, given the geography of the depression, this particularly affected the depressed areas of Wales, northern England and central Scotland, where life expectancy was shorter, the death rate was higher, and where maternal and infant mortality rates were the worst in the country. The evidence was fairly overwhelming, in other words, that health was primarily a matter of diet, and diet was primarily a matter of income.

National health insurance, introduced before 1914, was extended and broadened in stages between the wars to cover nineteen million people, but this provided only a small cash benefit while claimants were unfit for work, advice from a general practitioner and a rather rudimentary standard of treatment. Consultants' fees and hospitalization continued to be paid for out of private insurance schemes. Just as significantly, the scheme did not cover dependants. In the case of children, this was offset by the Board of Education's school medical inspections, but wives were simply not covered unless they worked and paid the insurance fee. Many working-class women could not afford to pay private insurance, with the result that a range of gynaecological and neurological complaints that could probably have been easily cured went without treatment or even medical advice, as women continued to suffer in silence. [DOCUMENT IX] There was a rise in the number of doctors and nurses per head of the population, but not a dramatic one. The number of hospital beds per head of the population rose only very little over the period. Given that members of the medical profession could earn a great deal more from their private patients than from 'panel' patients, there was no great incentive for them to establish practices in the poorer areas of the country, and it is clear that the medical services generally were inequitably distributed through Britain. The majority report of the Royal Commission on Health in 1926 recommended the extension of medical services whenever that was financially possible, but the minority report actually recommended the setting up of a National Health Service. This was taken up by the professional body, the British Medical Association, so that a key assumption of the Beveridge Report in 1942 did not emerge out of thin air; it emerged, rather, from developing professional opinion in the depression years about the best way to deal with the nation's health.

There is no question that health improved in virtually all areas between the wars, but there were no grounds for complacency. There were clear inequities in the health of the different social classes and different regions, and the system failed many women completely. On the other hand, it must be remembered that medical science was making great advances in the field of dietetics, which was revealing for the first time why some people were healthier than others. A problem cannot be rectified until it is properly identified. The wealth of material that we have available on the health of the nation between the wars was the product largely of that new breed of professional, the Chief Medical Officer. The introduction of a scientific and analytical survey of public health was the necessary preliminary for the political changes that were to come about in the next decade. What they showed was that the introduction of a National Health Service would not, in itself, be enough. Developing a healthy society depended not simply on doctors curing people but on the prevention of ill health, which in turn depended on a healthy diet, on education, and on everyone enjoying the standard of living and the quality of life that made sustained good health possible. That such an understanding should grow so rapidly is, in itself, a tribute to the distance Britain had travelled since the pre-war Liberal government had introduced the rather experimental idea of state health insurance for some of the population.

Education

There were fewer signs of social progress in education than in other areas. This was perhaps because education would not automatically improve with rising living standards, and was almost entirely dependent on state action. The essential block to progress in democratizing education lay with the privileged position of the grammar schools. The Local Education Authorities, established by the Conservatives in 1902 to take over the administration of education from the School Boards, had allowed great improvements in the education of children between the ages of 5 and 11, but they had also prevented the experiments that some School Boards had been working on to improve the education of those bright children who could not afford to go on to the fee-paying grammar schools. Further reform by the Liberal government later in the decade had introduced the scholarship scheme, which forced those grammar schools which were in receipt of state aid to take at least one-quarter of their intake from the state primary schools. The parents of those working-class children who were bright enough to win a place at grammar school, however, often found expenditure on uniform and other essentials a large burden. Quite apart from this, being part of a clear social minority in a school dominated by middle-class children was often a difficult experience. The 'scholarship boy' became a symbol of the alienating process of being born in one culture but educated in another.

One of the few positive results of Lloyd George's plans to introduce a great new programme of social legislation after the First World War was the Education Act of 1918, the work of H. A. L. Fisher. This raised the school-leaving age to fourteen and gave greater opportunities for working-class children to get into grammar school. Still, however, there were to be no real opportunities for those children who were not able to get into these schools. A great many of these children, indeed, seem to have simply spent three further years with the eleven-year-olds until the time came for them to leave, hardly a productive use of their time. In response, many elementary schools themselves began providing a separate secondary education, often very much more vocationally orientated than anything they would have got at grammar schools. In 1926, the Hadow Commission recommended that this system should become the general rule. It was, at least, a tacit recognition that children and young people had different needs and different abilities, that an inability to attain the academic qualifications that might come from a grammar-school education did not necessarily imply unfitness in other areas. Nor was it necessarily good for the nation's future that the ideals of the grammar schools, with their emphasis on the arts and humanities and pure sciences, should continue to dominate when it was clear that technical education lagged far behind that of Britain's industrial competitors. In turn, this self-reform by the elementary schools was to be expanded upon in the 1944 Education Act, which was primarily an attempt to establish equal but different forms of secondary education – grammar, technical and 'modern' – to meet the needs of different children.

Society and government between the wars: an overview

Improvements in social conditions in Britain between the wars came about mostly because of an improvement in the standard of living, itself a paradoxical function of a depression which forced down prices much more fully than wages or salaries. Government, it would seem, had far less to do with it. Yet the rapid rise in living standards of the large majority only threw into sharper relief the condition of that minority who were being left behind in the social advance. If the economy could not provide acceptable standards of living for all, then surely the state should have intervened more radically? Traditionally, the focus has been on the problem of unemployment. Perhaps the view that inter-war governments were hard-hearted and tight-fisted in their policy towards the unemployed is too harsh. Unemployment benefit had only covered some two million people when it had been introduced in 1911, and did not include many of those most at risk of losing their jobs; but it covered virtually everyone employed in Britain by 1939. The Special Areas Acts, however paltry the budgets attached to them from a post-1945 perspective, were serious experiments in job creation which flew in the face of the orthodoxy of a free labour market. And the cost of dealing with unemployment was, after all, one of the elements in precipitating the financial crisis of 1931. National governments in a global economy simply have to face the fact that international confidence is paramount, as overspending governments in the 1960s and 1970s had to relearn.

It was once argued by Bentley Gilbert, controversially, that Britain had acquired a welfare state in all but name by 1939. It would be more accurate to describe this period as a transitional stage between the original experiments of pre-1914 and the full-blown welfarism of post-1945. The numbers covered by unemployment and health insurance were vastly expanded and many of the blueprints of welfarism's basic projects had been at least drawn up, in the Minority Report of the Royal Commission on Health and the BMA's projection of the need for a National Health Service, in the research of the Hadow Commission, in the implications of the Special Areas Acts, in housing subsidies. Yet no commitment to using government policy to ensure, as nearly as possible, full employment, had been drawn up. Even more basic, there was as yet no overarching theory of welfarism as the duty of the state. Beveridge was to posit the twin principles of universality and comprehensiveness, the notions that everyone was collectively responsible for whatever misfortunes may befall anyone else. The changes made in social policy by inter-war governments did not draw inspiration from such a powerful notion of a contract drawn up between nation and state; they were, rather, piecemeal and *ad hoc* reactions to prevailing circumstances.

The fact is that Britain suffered much less obvious political unrest from unemployment than did other countries, and the relatively generous benefits given out in Britain may account for this, at least in part. Another possible reason for the relative lack of social friction, however, had nothing to do with the action or inaction of government. In Britain, unemployment was not only relatively lower than in other countries; it was also much more localized. In their study of the long-term unemployed, the Pilgrim Trust found that in the depressed areas, the areas of highest unemployment, there was typically a sense of fatalistic acceptance because everyone was in the same boat. It was in the areas of relatively low unemployment, where the sense of relative deprivation was greater, that more militant reactions were to be found. [**DOCUMENT V**] It may be, then, that militancy tended to be confined to a small minority of the minority who were unemployed. Undoubtedly, too, the rise in the numbers of the lower middle class, and the establishment of their territory in suburbia, did much to stabilize the situation. Unlike their opposite numbers in

Germany, who were financially ruined by the hyperinflation of the 1920s and who appear to have turned in droves to Fascism, the British lower middle class seemed perfectly happy to tend their new gardens. This was a depression that not only made most people richer; it also put into social ghettos the groups that caused most problems in other countries. True, the ghettoization was not exactly a positive process, in that one ghetto was characterized by a degree of self-satisfaction and the other by rather fatalistic attitudes, but it may just have helped a little to preserve the peace.

4.   Cultures: Leisure in the Depression

People were not only better off during the inter-war years; they were also working fewer hours and having more time for leisure. For some, of course, the extra leisure was unwanted and difficult to contend with. The long-term unemployed had less rather than more money to spend, and had only restricted access to the forms of mass leisure which were becoming available to the majority. For those in work, however, there was an average reduction in the working week from 54 hours before the First World War to 48 in the early 1920s. While there was little further reduction in the inter-war period, as firms tended to shed workers but expect more from those they continued to employ, there was legislation to prevent over-long hours in the Shops Act of 1934 and the Factories Act of 1937, which limited working hours to 48 in those industries where excessive overtime was being worked. The Holidays with Pay Act of 1938 increased the number of workers guaranteed statutory holidays from one to four million, though many more were covered by voluntary agreements within their industry.

Spare time is just as important to historians as work time. Most people work to live, after all, not live to work. Work provides money for subsistence, but also money to enjoy oneself. The typical leisure patterns of the past are, therefore, potentially significant indicators of what people wanted to do, rather than what they had to do. This is not to say that leisure is completely separated from work, because work constrains leisure in many important ways. Work dictates the periods of the day and the times of year when leisure may be taken, but work also makes people members of one social class rather than another. Traditionally, the different social classes have enjoyed their leisure in different typical ways. For the large majority of women, moreover, the distinction between work and leisure is, historically, much less clear-cut than it is for men. Women in paid work, particularly if they have families, have rarely expected to go from

'work' to 'leisure' when they go home; there have always been domestic responsibilities over and above their paid work. For housewives who do not go out to work, men's leisure time tends to increase
domestic responsibilities rather than lessen them; in a typical
patriarchal family, there is more cooking and cleaning to do, and less
control of the work environment in the home, when men are not at
work. Many housewives included in their 'leisure' pursuits sewing
and mending clothes, lending credence to the cliché that 'a woman's
work is never done'. Leisure, then, is to a large extent defined by its
supposed opposite, work, but differently for men and for women, and
differently for the social classes.

Increasing leisure and increasing affluence were to mean that leisure
in itself became a profitable industry, and a new source of
employment. A hundred thousand were already employed in entertainment and sport by 1920; by 1938, this had increased to 247,000,
besides the 494,000 employed in catering and hotels. The commercialization of leisure, already increasingly apparent in the late nineteenth
century, was a major aspect of spare-time activity in inter-war Britain,
most noticeably of all in cinema, but also in holiday-making and in
sport. Making profits from leisure involves, of course, appealing to as
many people as possible. It tends therefore to be a homogenizing
influence, appealing across class, gender, regional and even national
boundaries. What we tend to see in inter-war British leisure patterns, as
a result, is a series of unconscious negotiations which tended to undermine some of the traditional sharp distinctions in class, regional and
national identities, and the negotiation of new gender identities more
in tune with an affluent, modernist age.

Family, hearth and home

The enormous development in home-building of this period
provided comfortable houses and home environments for a large
section of the population. As a result, there was much more of an
incentive to enjoy home-based pursuits, particularly among the 45
per cent of families who were owner-occupiers or council tenants by
the end of the 1930s. The pub declined as a centre of community
leisure, and with it the range of pursuits that had been associated
with the pub and its spin-off, the music hall, in the Victorian era.
Popular music, for example, was transformed by the gramophone,
for the better-off at least, and by the radio, available to more than 75

per cent of all families by the mid-1930s. There was certainly a boom in dance-halls in the 1920s but, increasingly, people did not have to go out to hear either music or variety entertainment. The gramophone and the radio provided a highly professional product which could be enjoyed at home. Undoubtedly, the domestication of popular music also involved a standardization. While BBC radio could encourage the development of British talent, and made household names of dance-band leaders like Henry Hall, as well as other popular entertainers like Arthur Askey, this may well have been at the expense of local entertainers and regional talents who could not hope to compete. Popular music, moreover, became one of the most obvious early avenues for the 'Americanization' of British popular culture in general. Domestication and standardization did not necessarily devalue popular culture, as critics of mass society believed, but they certainly changed it. 'Mass culture' involved leaving less room for regional variations and transformed popular culture into something to be consumed rather than something in which one participated, as one did in a live performance.

Along with better home environments went the development of home improvement and gardening as typical leisure routines. The low-density building on the new estates not only gave families more space; it also increased the attractions of privacy and of a more introverted, family-based rather than community-based way of life. The extended family became less significant and the nuclear family more central as young adults increasingly set up house not next door, nor in the next street, but in a suburban estate. The effect of this was more important for women than it was for men. Women traditionally relied upon the female members of the extended family network for education in householding and in rearing a family, for help with emotional and 'women's' problems, as well as help with child-minding and domestic work. Increasingly, married women were to become housebound, reliant on other forms of information such as advice columns in newspapers, or magazines specifically geared to the new housewife; *Woman, Woman's Own, Good Housekeeping* and *Women's Journal* all began publication in this period, providing populist, colourful and entertaining education in femininity. **[DOCUMENT XI]** Advertising increasingly centred on the young housewife as a prime target in the consumer economy. Household tools such as electric ovens and vacuum cleaners were marketed as if they were leisure items for women, while cheaper cosmetics and clothes encouraged younger women not to become the drudges their mothers had been. The accent was on the way that fewer children, labour-saving devices and the democratization of glamour gave women the 'leisure' to be more caring mothers and more attractive wives.

Holidays away from home increasingly centred on the family rather than the work-related 'wakes' weeks or firm excursions. While men going on holiday with other men they worked with, with or without their families, had reinforced the gender ties of work, the holiday of the nuclear family on its own underlined the new ideology of domesticity. The holiday camps – Butlin's were the most successful – were the most obvious examples of the new mass holiday market, specifically geared to families with young children. The seaside resorts also increasingly geared themselves to young families, providing new entertainment centres, Dreamland in Margate for example, or the Blackpool Pleasure Beach. In turn, the availability of cheap and easy-to-use cameras provided holiday snapshots for the family album, the first reliable evidence most families had of their own development, and increasingly iconographic. This is not to say that better housing and cheap holidays eroded the gap between the social classes. Owner-occupiers and council tenants may have listened to the same radio programmes, but housing estates were sharply delineated into class ghettos; so, too, were venues for holidays, as the better-off increasingly looked to go abroad to avoid the masses. The point is, however, that the ideology of domesticity and the centrality of the family during leisure time, which had previously typified only the middle class, was now increasingly typical of the better-paid working class.

For poorer working-class families, however, domesticity was not an option. In the inner-city areas of the north, Scotland and south Wales, the street and the pub retained their appeal for much longer than in the newly prosperous areas. Children still played marbles, hopscotch, and cricket with an upturned box as a wicket in the street well into the 1950s in these areas, eschewing publicly-provided parks, which were intended for quiet and respectable family excursions. Families from such areas, moved by slum clearance to more spacious surroundings in another area, frequently missed the hum and chatter of the old communities, and hankered after the mutual support of the traditional working-class networks. But the physical destruction of the old environment, so important for improvements in health as well as to provide other opportunities, necessarily involved the destruction of older loyalties. Homes built to house families, as opposed to

tenements or back-to-backs built to house the working class, involved
nothing less than a different way of looking at the world.

Unemployment and regional identity

Unemployment was concentrated in the areas of Britain whose
identity was fixed by the heavy industries which dominated their
economy. Without alternative sources of employment, these areas
went into spiralling depression. With less money in the area, local
authorities were not able to repair roads, small shops were not able to
stay open and younger people left the region. Although government
began to intervene in a small way to rejuvenate the depressed areas,
by and large these areas had to make do with the mutual-support
mechanisms that they had developed in slightly rosier days, or else
accepted the charitable support of organizations like the National
Council of Social Service. Although attempts were made to radicalize
the areas politically, these attempts appear to have been largely
unsuccessful. The problem appears to have been that the heart went
out of a culture, a way of life, that had been built so fundamentally
on sheer hard physical work, in the pits and in the furnaces. Yet, in
the writing and other cultural work of working-class and middle-class
intellectuals, the depressed areas were to have their revenge, for the
legacy of unemployment was to damn the inter-war years in the
popular imagination for more than thirty years after 1939.

Where work was physically the hardest, patriarchy tended to be
most fully developed. In coal-mining, for example, where women had
been banned from pit work for many generations, and where the
danger of work below ground bred a particularly strong male
solidarity, unemployment was a spiritually emasculating experience.
In the south Wales coalfield, the distinctive culture of the miners'
world had been further delineated by the coming together of English
immigrants and migrants from west Wales, forming an Anglo-Welsh
identity in the nineteenth century, distinct both from the English to
the east and the Welsh-speaking agricultural communities to the
north and west. A similarly distinct identity marked the coal-mining
communities of Scotland. The Miners' Institutes undoubtedly
provided a lifeline when unemployment struck. The Mining Industry
Act of 1920 created a fund to modernize and improve leisure
facilities in the Institutes. Of this welfare fund £1.25 million was
spent in south Wales alone, not that far short of what government

made available for all the depressed areas in Britain under the Special Areas Act. The institutes got men out of their homes, where they probably often felt uncomfortable, and provided centres for sports, education and politics, as well as practice rooms for those distinctive musical forms, the pipe bands in Scotland and the male-voice choirs in Wales.

The working men's clubs performed similar functions in other areas of industry, especially in northern England. They preserved a traditional working-class identity where the rationale for such an identity, work, had disappeared. They were political, in the sense that they were democratically run and imbued with a definite socialist spirit, but they were rarely radicalized. Miners appear to have been more internationally-minded than other members of the British working class; the south Wales miners in particular saw a sizeable contingent go to Spain to fight for the Republicans. In small pockets, too, radicalism did flourish, such as in Mardy, the 'Little Moscow' of the Rhondda valleys, where mourners at funerals sang the International over wreaths shaped as hammers and sickles. More often than not, however, the working-class networks that kept the unemployed communities together, reflected a solidarity that was non-combative, accepting that virtually everybody in the community was in the same boat, [DOCUMENT V] and confident that a socialist presence in a parliamentary democracy would eventually bring about a fairer society. This was just as well, for the police and Home Office were prepared to use their powers to prevent any hint of insurrectionism. There certainly were violent demonstrations by the unemployed during the period, but they were rarely publicized, because reporting restrictions were imposed. Indeed, the most famous demonstration of the period, the Jarrow Crusade, went ahead only because the organizers promised a peaceful march and co-operated with the police.

It might be said, too, that the national projection of the depressed areas was patronizing, to modern eyes at least. The Prince of Wales's role as patron of the National Council of Social Service attracted the newsreel companies to film him in south Wales or in County Durham, and to feature him as the king-to-be with the common touch, the friend of the working man. When feature film touched on unemployment or the depressed areas, it invariably pictured stoical communities, heroicized by their fatalistic acceptance of their lot. *Proud Valley*, for example, set in south Wales, had the mining community bursting into yet another hymn as each new disaster struck. Literary projections of unemployment and poverty were not always more radical. J. B. Priestley gave a graphic enough account of the depressed areas in his *English Journey*, but did so in a context which emphasized that the depressed areas were only one of the faces of England, and not the dominant one. **[DOCUMENT XII]** George Orwell tried to communicate the experience of poverty in the north of England for a southern, affluent public in *The Road to Wigan Pier* but, published by the Left Book Club, he was preaching to a small and converted audience. From the depressed areas themselves, however, came alternative projections which, in the changed political climate of the 1940s and 1950s, were to come to be seen as more representative of the period than suburbia and affluence. Bert Coombs's *These Poor Hands*, Walter Greenwood's *Love on the Dole* and Lewis Grassic Gibbon's *A Scots Quair* were novels which not only depicted the grinding demoralization associated with unemployment and poverty, but did so from a specifically regional perspective.

Sport and the great outdoors

Although cricket enjoyed one of its most popular periods between the wars, it was football which was the dominant sport. Football had become the national working-class game in the late nineteenth century. In the northern towns of England and in the central Lowlands of Scotland, the local football team was just as much a source of civic pride for the working class as the building of majestic town halls had been for the middle class earlier in the century. Imported from the public schools to teach the working class the values of combining personal skill with team spirit and self-discipline, the game blossomed. By the end of the century, the increasing professionalization of football had virtually excluded middle-class players and spectators. During the inter-war years, professional sport grew more commercialized but, as in so many other areas of the inter-war experience, fortunes tended to reflect economic conditions. Where northern football teams had prospered in the 1890s, southern teams were increasingly able to put a good deal of capital into the transfer market and into attractive new stadia. Successful teams were the ones that saw the need to switch attention to the managerial needs of what had now become an industry. Thus, formerly ascendant teams like Preston North End, Blackburn Rovers and Newcastle United were in relative decline in the 1930s, while

Arsenal dominated. The success or failure of the local football team may have more or less reflected the economic well-being of the area, but at least the relative lack of success of the northern teams was offset in national pride at the continuing international success of the England team. Rugby Union in Wales, on the other hand, rampant against England before the First World War, declined as key players were lost to the professional Rugby League, whereas English Rugby Union was much less reliant on working-class players who would feel the financial pinch in a depression. Football and rugby, in other words, articulated and reflected both local and national working-class fortunes.

Increasingly, however, football managers strove to provide, and spectators came to expect, spectacular skill and success rather than simply 'playing the game'. In 1908/9, it has been calculated that six million watched First Division matches in England, with an average crowd of about 16,000. In 1937/8, 31.5 million watched Football League matches in England in all, but no fewer than 14 million of these were watching First Division matches, with an average crowd of 30,000. This was an area in which working-class male solidarity flourished. Visual evidence of the crowds at football matches from this period shows the game to be a wholly male preserve, and shows too the striking uniform of cloth cap and muffler which did so much to disguise differences of age or region among the working class. While photographs of working-class men before 1914 reveal fine social gradations in the dress of a skilled artisan or a labourer, photographs and movies from between the wars show a far more homogenized, 'identikit' picture. The teams they were watching were also, still, working-class in terms of income. The maximum wage enforced by the Football League until the 1960s was substantially above that open to most workers but, even in the First Division, only the first team at the more successful clubs could expect to be paid at the top end of the scale. The career of a football player was so short, moreover, that life-time earnings may not have exceeded by much that of the best-paid workers in industry. The stars of this particular corner of the leisure industry, then, were not the remote figures heard on radio or seen on the cinema screen. These were real people you could watch on a Saturday, and they remained, in class terms, 'one of us'. The football pools also encouraged participation in the sport, in the sense that success did depend at least in part on skill in forecasting results. For a very small outlay, one could at least dream about riches and display one's knowledge of the game.

Perhaps one major reason why professional football remained relatively impervious to the standardizing trend in inter-war culture was that, until 1935, the BBC rarely broadcast live commentary. The Corporation had been initially dubious about the educative content of professional sport and, in that perverse anti-populist stance that so often characterized John Reith's reign at the BBC, actually preferred to broadcast amateur football (a game for the absolutely devoted spectator, surely). There was also worry from the football clubs that live commentary would lead to falling gates and an increasing concentration only on the most successful clubs. From the mid-1930s, however, the Cup Final became a national institution to which millions tuned in to hear Raymond Glendenning's commentary, an intrinsic part of the BBC's projection of Britain back to the British people. Internationals and Cup semi-finals also became part of the BBC's regular output. Thus, a sport that was truly working-class continued to be articulated to a national, cross-class identity.

It is clear, however, that football was growing as a players' game and not just as a spectator sport. The metropolitan boroughs of London kept available 1,816 acres of sports playing-fields in 1927. In Liverpool there were 172 football pitches. There is clear evidence of a developing interest not only in playing team sports but in physical fitness generally, and in fresh-air pursuits. Cycling, already established as the working man's way to work, also became a leisure pursuit. Cars may have been available to the very affluent, but bicycles were available to everyone. In 1920 385,000 bicycles were sold, but by 1935 sales had increased to 1.6 million. The two largest cycling clubs had 60,000 members between them by 1938. The Youth Hostel Association went through startling growth, from 6,439 members in 1930 to 79,821 in 1938. There is no doubt that outdoor pursuits tended to be dominated by middle-class participants but there was increasing interest from working-class people, even though they often felt socially ostracized. The claustrophobia of the inner cities and the threat of suburban sprawl obviously stimulated this new interest in the countryside. By the mid-1930s, there were growing demands for protection of the countryside and increased access to the great outdoors by urban dwellers. The London County Council was planning for the first green belt around the capital, while the mass trespass on Kinder Scout in Derbyshire attracted press support for some clearer legal definition of public rights of way, and contributed to the moves behind the Access to Mountains Act of 1939. It was in the last year of peace, too, that Britain's first National Park was opened.

While team sports, whether watching or playing them, were wholly dominated by men, the development of other outdoor pursuits saw a much fuller participation from women. Certainly, that participation tended to be expressed in terms of domesticity. For most women, after all, the country walk was either part of the ritual of courtship or a family outing. Nevertheless, the fact was that women as well as men were benefiting not just from fresh air, but from the healthy perspective on life that being out of the city and out of the home put on the everyday world. The notion that there was another world beyond work and the city, a place continually projected as the common heritage, the countryside, undoubtedly provided another source of belief that national identity was at least as significant as class or gender identity.

Cinema

Football is a seasonal game, of course, while cinema is available the year round: but it is worth pointing out that for every one person who went to a football match in 1938, thirty went to the cinema. For cinema, this was the golden age. In 1938, 987 million tickets were sold, a gross take of £41.5 million. The average weekly audience by the late 1930s was between 17 and 19 million. It was not simply the films that attracted the audiences, though, clearly, if the films had generally failed to impress, the audiences would have stopped going. But cinema was a night out, and the film was only part of the entertainment. It was, first of all, a very cheap night out, and in buildings which ranged from extravagant rococo to state-of-the-art modernism. In the latter category was the distinctive Odeon chain of cinemas, at the very cutting edge of progressive architecture in this period, with their cream-tiled, stream-lined exteriors and unmistakable red neon signs. Inside were art deco lights and plush seating, Wurlitzer organs and cheap meals or snacks in pleasant cafés. Inside, too, was the warmest dark place for courting couples. Surveys of the time show that the young working class were the most avid cinema-goers. This was particularly true among the young unemployed, the Carnegie Trust finding that about 80 per cent of this group went to the cinema at least once a week. Married working-class women also made up a large part of those who went to the cinema at least once a week, but one survey in 1934 suggested that 40 per cent of the total population of Merseyside went to the cinema every week, and that 25 per cent went twice a week or more.

Although cinema-going was more frequent among the working class, those higher up the social scale seem to have lost their initial condescending attitude, so that, by the 1930s, it was a major leisure activity of the middle class as well. Audience reaction to films varied according to the social class of the audience and the region. Cinema managers, who had good reason to do the research, found that working-class audiences much preferred American films to British, finding the lack of action and the staginess of the latter boring. Scottish and Welsh working-class audiences found British films simply patronizing, and had more problems deciphering the middle-class accents of English film actors than they did those of, say, the Marx Brothers. Mixed, family audiences preferred light comedies and romances, an American film starring a British actor for instance, but not a British film starring an American actor, which they felt was a British film trying to be American and failing. Middle-class audiences, on the other hand, had a definite preference for British films, finding American films brash, violent and loud. [DOCUMENT XIII] Such different reactions make it difficult to come to catch-all judgements on the impact of film. Certainly, one should not conclude that it was simple propaganda which brainwashed the British through the depression. Different audiences negotiated different films in different ways. They accepted what they liked from the menu, and rejected what they did not like.

British film had a hard time competing with Hollywood, on the whole. At the same time, the films of Gracie Fields and George Formby were clearly very popular, especially with family audiences. Fields's films combined musical with social comedy, and projected stoicism and humour as typical attributes of the Lancastrian working class, whether faced with unemployment, as in *Sing As We Go* ('as long as you smile, then your life's worthwhile'), or cross-class relationships, as in *Sally in our Alley* ('your lordship, er . . . worship, I mean your ladyship'). These films inherited from the music hall and developed what the social historian Gareth Stedman Jones called a 'culture of consolation'; economic disaster was inevitable for the working class, but they could always have a good laugh and thumb their noses at the establishment. Formby, the gormless but good-natured ukulele player, normally relied on the basic decency of the community to save him from the machinations of villains and from his own inadequacy. His films celebrated a British sense of fair play. [DOCUMENT XIV] Things 'turned out nice again' because fair play demanded that the good-natured underdog should have his day.

There was no sense of social criticism in these films. Although they celebrated the working class, what they celebrated about the working class was its Britishness: fair-minded, humorous, unpretentious, fatalistic and proud to be just a little bit stupid. Politically minded film reviewers despaired at the popularity of such films, but the fact is that they built on a very popular and firmly established representation of the working class, with which working-class people seem to have felt comfortable. Towards the end of the period, however, a small number of films appeared that did look forward to the kind of political change that was to come about during the Second World War. Among these were *The Citadel,* about the need for reform of health care, and *The Stars Look Down*, an argument for the nationalization of the mines. What was significant about such films, however, was that there was only a handful of them. The arguments they made, moreover, were again couched specifically in terms of British fair play. And the arguments were made not by working-class people but by doctors (*The Citadel*) or *déclassé* scholarship boys (*The Stars Look Down*), while their working-class audiences on film could only listen and wonder.

British film was, of course, subject to heavy censorship, which would have forbidden any extensive comment on the political, social or moral *status quo*. American film had to deal with a censorship code that was just as strict, however, yet still managed to make more exciting films. The gangster genre portrayed poor immigrants to America not in the stoic fashion that British film represented the British working class, but as tough and self-preserving. Even if they did eventually fail, these boys from the slums went down fighting. There can be little wonder that most male working-class youths, though they might laugh at/with George Formby, preferred James Cagney as a role model. American musicals far outshone their British counterparts, Fred Astaire and Ginger Rogers providing a ritualization of romantic love that made the British and very middle-class Jessie Matthews look prosaic. What American film projected was a 'can-do', cosmopolitan society, where people could get on. What British film projected was a class-ridden and emotionally constrained society. American film was prepared to project a new kind of woman, too, in the aggressive Bette Davis, the scheming Joan Crawford and the sexually adventurous Greta Garbo. Certainly, these new women were all put firmly in their place by the end of the film, but at least a statement had been made. They tended to come back, too, in the same kind of role next month.

Hollywood was, in fact, remarkably kind to Britain and probably projected British values rather better than did British cinema. A large number of British actors were bought up by the American studios to play languidly romantic leading men, Leslie Howard for example, or quiet gentlemanly heroes, of whom the doyen was Ronald Colman. While British cinema made a number of forays into national history, producing stately re-enactments of the life of *The Iron Duke* or *Victoria the Great*, Hollywood turned British imperial history into a sub-genre of the Western. For Hollywood, the British Empire was a swashbuckling romp from *Lives of a Bengal Lancer* to *Gunga Din*. Even when they dealt with real events, these films were unencumbered either by the facts about the past (the Charge of the Light Brigade took place on the North-West Frontier, according to Hollywood) or any sense of the 'white man's burden', which afflicted the British so much in their own rather stodgy cinematic treatment of Empire. In an age when educational provision was so inadequate, it is possible that most young working-class people learned their history in the cinema. If so, they must have been extremely proud of their country, for there was never even a hint of criticism in these films.

While it would be simplistic to argue that audiences' attitudes were shaped by what they saw in the cinema, the very commercial success of cinema suggests that audiences liked what they saw. If working-class audiences did not like the poshness and the politeness of so much home-produced material, they did not object either to the lack of social comment or to what later generations might see as a patronizing projection of working people by Gracie Fields and George Formby. Far from objecting, they made them the biggest British box-office stars of the 1930s. From America, too, they got images of an open and progressive society, which they might have contrasted with their own, but they also received a flattering depiction of Anglo-Saxon masculinity, as well as an exciting picture of British history. There was nothing to worry audiences, in short, that their country was not sound at heart.

Culture and the state

While many cultural commentators railed against the new mass culture and its most obvious manifestation in cinema, government was mainly concerned only that it should not have political repercussions. It says something about the perceived power of cinema, however, and worries about the process of 'Americanization' of Britain, that government abandoned its free-trade policy as early as 1927 to save the British film industry. The Cinematograph Films Act decreed that a quota of films shown in Britain must be British-made, rising gradually to 20 per cent by 1933. Although this may have saved an industry in deep trouble from American competition, the legislation had other, less helpful, repercussions. The Act encouraged the production of low-budget 'quota quickies' which no doubt contributed substantially to British cinema's reputation for awfulness among working-class audiences. On the whole, however, government could expect the producers of culture to police themselves. The British Board of Film Censors, for example, was never an official government body; it was a self-regulating body maintained by the film industry. The BBFC, however, could be relied upon to wield the blue pencil however potentially profitable a film project might be. Working to a strict set of rules which forbade scenes likely to endanger morality or promote civil unrest, either at home or in the Empire, the BBFC worked in a subtle way. For financial reasons, it was helpful for producers to know early in a project whether a film was likely to be censored, so the BBFC began accepting outline proposals and commenting upon them. More often than not, as a result, films did not get censored, they simply never got started. *Love on the Dole* was accepted as material fit for a novel-reading audience in 1931, but was rejected twice as a film scenario by the BBFC in the 1930s. One can only conclude that the BBFC simply did not trust the largely working-class cinema audience to react in the same way as the largely middle-class novel-reading audience.

The BBC was also an autonomous organization, though ultimate responsibility for the effective running of this first public corporation rested with the state. Like the BBFC, however, it would always have to work on the assumption that, if it did not regulate itself in ways acceptable to the government, it could expect intervention. The BBC was also entirely dependent financially upon the state to maintain the licence fee. Although John Reith, director general of the BBC, had to act firmly to maintain the independence of the Corporation during the General Strike, it was never seriously in doubt thereafter. Indeed, inter-war radio was criticized for bias as much from the right as from the left. There is no doubt, however, that the BBC was conservative-minded. Reith saw radio as having primarily an educative role.

Although radio clearly did make American popular music widely available, and pioneered a style of light entertainment that for two generations produced comedy series with a huge popular following, Reith would have seen the contribution of radio drama and the formation of the BBC Symphony Orchestra as much more important. Radio also made news available faster than ever before, most famously in the prime minister's announcement of the declaration of war on Germany at 11.15 a.m. on 3 September 1939. Above all, perhaps, it was the measured tones of news readers which established 'BBC English' as 'the voice of Britain'. Only in wartime did the BBC resort to a more populist approach and allow regional accents on to the air, those of J. B. Priestley and Wilfred Pickles, most famously, though even their accents were highly mediated.

Government was not above using sport for international political purposes. Perhaps this was unavoidable, given the popularity of international sport. The 'bodyline' cricket tour of Australia in the 1930s caused ructions in the Empire, with or without government intervention. Where politics was paramount, government was often transparent in its attitude. The Labour government in 1930 refused to grant entry visas to a Soviet football team on a tour organized by the British Workers' Sports Federation because, as the Home Secretary put it, there was no evidence that genuine sport was the object. The government was clearly worried that, as had happened in France a few years previously, the Russian side would go on to the pitch waving the Red Flag and singing the 'International'. Different treatment faced teams from right-wing countries. Government refused to intervene when TUC and anti-Fascist organizations protested against the German national side's appearance against England at White Hart Lane in 1935, even though it was well known that Tottenham Hotspurs had a particularly large number of Jewish supporters. Indeed, the choice of venue seemed almost deliberately offensive. When the England team visited Berlin in 1938, moreover, the Foreign Office put pressure on the England players to give the Nazi salute during the German national anthem, the photographs of which were later to become enduring images of Britain's humiliation by appeasement.

Nevertheless, the state encouraged local authorities to develop their recreational amenities. The large number of sporting pitches available in British cities was testimony to this, and local authorities bowed to pressure to allow sport on Sundays in public parks. The local authorities also contributed substantially to an increase in reading as a spare-time activity. The number of registered readers in public libraries rose from 2.6 million in 1924 to 8.9 in 1939, and the number of books borrowed rose from 85.6 to 247 million. Never before had there been such a range of leisure opportunities available, and never before had the state, at national and local level, taken such an interest in providing them. While the commercialization and standardization of leisure may have started to break down regional differences in Britain, while mass culture may have begun to challenge popular culture – a culture genuinely of, by and for the people – people still had choices. The vast majority could choose to turn off the radio and read a library book. They could choose to spend a few pence on a British or an American film, or go for a walk in a public park. A larger number of men than ever before could choose to tend their gardens or watch or play football, or go out with their families in the countryside. Certainly, the range of leisure opportunities for the unemployed and the poor was less than for others. Certainly, too, leisure patterns remained deeply gendered. The fact remains that few chose to take the opportunity of increased leisure to develop a challenge to dominant modes of thinking. The few who did watch the Russian revolutionary feature films in film clubs, who read the editions of the Left Book Club or the new proletarian novelists, had to wait until a new political and social context emerged in 1940 to take them from the periphery into the mainstream of British culture.

5.   The Structure of Politics

The first sixteen years of the twentieth century saw all the major political parties in Britain faced with crisis. For the Liberals, the twenty years before their electoral victory in 1906 had seen the party split by the question of Irish Home Rule, and upstaged by the imperialist stance of the Conservatives. They had also been worried by the emergence of a Labour party which threatened the future of the alliance between middle-class and working-class interests on which their electoral success depended. Although an agreement with the Labour party was concluded just before the 1906 election, and although the programme of social reforms they put through Parliament in subsequent years might have confirmed that alliance, the elections of 1910 made them once again reliant on the votes of the Irish Nationalists, as they had been in 1885 and 1892. Embroiled in another Home Rule Bill, and having to reform the House of Lords in order to push Home Rule through, the Liberal government then stumbled into a war that it was not ideologically suited to run. The emergence of Lloyd George as the man prepared to take the state action necessary to win the war, and his increasing comfort with Conservatives as allies, set the party up for the disastrous split that was confirmed in the election of 1918. The Conservatives may have been saved by the war from their own disastrous split over tariff reform and their irresponsible behaviour over Home Rule and House of Lords reform, but they were by no means certain of their future in a world of revolution abroad and mass democracy at home. Labour had not been able to make a decisive electoral breakthrough before 1914 and, in a Lloyd George coalition with the Tories from 1916, were faced with an alliance of the centre and right which might prove electorally devastating.

The state of flux into which British politics was thrust in the era of the Irish question and the First World War might have led to a situation in which extremist political groupings could take advantage.

In fact, the period proved to be only one of transition from one two-party system to another. Fundamentally, the failure of either the extreme right or the extreme left to gain any more than the merest toehold in Britain was the result of economic, social and cultural forces which have already been described. But part of the reason for the durability of the political system in Britain was the manœuvring of political leaders to maintain two great coalitions, one of the left and one of the right, both led from the centre. The end of the Irish question in 1922, moreover, calmed many of the cross-party frictions that had disturbed politics heavily since the 1880s.

Baldwin and conservatism

The major reason the Conservatives agreed to go into the general election of 1918 in coalition with Lloyd George was because they were not at all sure they could win without 'the man who had won the war'. The great populist war leader appeared the ideal personality to lead the attack on the socialist challenge that must come with the Representation of the People Act of 1918, which promised universal manhood suffrage and a limited vote for women, and an electorate in which the working class would dominate for the first time. It was agreed for the 'Coupon election' that Lloyd George's supporters would not fight Conservatives, and that Conservatives would also give the Lloyd George Liberals a free run. In fact, the 1918 election was a triumph for the Conservatives. Although Lloyd George managed to retain a small parliamentary base with the Coalition Liberals, it was increasingly clear to a section of the Tories that they did not need Lloyd George. The coalition came unstuck over social and financial policy as the depression struck in 1920 and 1921. The Coalition Liberals were forced to accept cuts in public expenditure which ruined their hopes for post-war social reform, and they drifted back to the rump of the Liberal party. Then, in 1922, when Lloyd George took the country to the brink of war in the Chanak crisis, the backbenchers of the Tory party revolted. Their spokesman was Stanley Baldwin, and his argument was that Lloyd George was a 'dynamic force' who would end up destroying the Conservative party just as effectively as he had destroyed the Liberals. Although the leaders of the Tories were still of the opinion that Lloyd George was the only man who could stop socialism, Baldwin felt that the Conservatives could do it on their own.

In the ensuing election in 1922, however, there were some signs that the Tory leaders might be right, as the Conservative vote dropped below 40 per cent of the popular vote for the first time in nearly forty years. It was only the fact that their opponents were too divided that allowed the Conservatives to form a government. In spite of nervousness about him, Stanley Baldwin succeeded to the leadership with the illness of Andrew Bonar Law, but worries about his political acumen among Tory grandees were not laid to rest. Indeed, when he opted for an election manifesto suggesting tariff reform as an answer to the current economic problems, he let in the first Labour government in the election of December 1923. Having thus proved that tariff reform was still an electoral liability, he brought in the free-trading renegade Winston Churchill as Chancellor of the Exchequer in his next government at the end of 1924.

This apparent shallowness in Baldwin's ideological outlook and beliefs in fact disguised a consummate politician. He placed himself and his party deliberately outside the realm of the 'dynamic forces' like Lloyd George, and patrician intellectuals such as Lord Birkenhead, and plumped for ordinariness. He distanced himself from those 'grey faced men' he saw in the House of Commons in 1918, 'who looked as though they had done well out of the war'. He also claimed, at least in retrospect, that his strategy between 1922 and 1924 had been deliberate. He had taken on tariff reform, he later implied, to ensure that Conservatives did not drift off to Lloyd George. Having thus forced Lloyd George to distance himself from possible Tory support in 1923, he had then brought back Winston Churchill in 1924 to attract right-wing Liberal support. He claimed that his aim had been to create one broad alliance of the right, in the Conservative party, by destroying Lloyd George and further weakening the Liberals. While Lord Birkenhead thought that the Conservatives had to 'resist socialism or perish', Baldwin realized that Labour were not Bolsheviks and that a populist stance, with limited social reform when it was financially possible, was the best way of easing the country into the new age. Further electoral reform, giving women the vote on the same basis as men in 1928, would prove that the Conservatives could run with democracy, not fight it. Baldwin's leadership was often under threat. While Churchill provided financial orthodoxy at the Exchequer in the second half of the 1920s, the Chancellor's aggression towards organized labour created difficulties in the General Strike; neither could he be held in check when Baldwin seemed ready to discuss the possibility of at least loosening the ties with India in the early 1930s. The press barons continued to despise Baldwin, moreover, Beaverbrook launching another campaign for imperial tariff reform in the early 1930s which was aimed at removing Baldwin from the leadership. Having replied with the stinging rebuke that the press had power without responsibility, 'the prerogative of the harlot', Baldwin then sat and watched as Neville Chamberlain introduced tariff reform with imperial preference.

Although Baldwin's leadership was never unchallenged, he rode the challenges with ease. His slogan 'Safety first' clearly chimed well with an electorate worried by the depression but, as we have seen, not suffering too severely, except in regionally limited areas. He was no doubt lucky, too, that the most serious repercussions of the inter-war financial crisis fell not on one of his administrations, but on one of Labour's. In the 1931 financial crisis, his stance was not to make huge political capital out of Labour's failures but to offer coalition, with the Labour leader continuing as prime minister. The result of the election of 1931 was as clearly a victory for the Conservatives as had been the coalition election of 1918, and it left the Tories in complete political command in the thirties. This willingness of the Conservatives to continue the coalition in 1918, to create a 'National Government' in 1931 and continue it in 1935, made it easy to suggest that the Conservatives truly were the party with the national interest at heart. Baldwin had even managed to give the impression that the ending of the coalition in 1922 had been necessary to save the national interest from a dynamic force. Either way, in making or breaking coalitions, the Conservatives came out on top as the party of 'Safety first', while their opponents appeared to represent sectional interest or dangerous experiment.

Baldwin's other famous slogan, 'give peace in our time', has often been associated with his attitudes to foreign policy. In fact, it was originally an appeal for industrial peace, made in 1925 as the crisis in the coal industry developed. While the policies of his government – decontrol of the coal industry and the return to the Gold Standard – were hardly designed to avoid confrontation, and even the right-wing Lord Birkenhead thought the coal owners 'the stupidest men in England', Baldwin was prepared to see the General Strike through as a battle for democracy between an elected government and sectional interests. Yet Baldwin constantly emphasized the value of negotiation over confrontation, of honest toil over selfishness, and appealed to the supposed basic decency of 'deep England'. His book of essays and speeches, *On England*, stressed the harmonious tradition of the English countryside, suggesting that this was an England just as real and just as meaningful as that of inner cities and industrial un- employment. [DOCUMENT XV]

Baldwin was also the first politician to see the significance of the new mass media in communicating to the vastly expanded electorate. Conservative Central Office courted both the BBC and the cinema newsreel companies and, while Baldwin was a significant radio performer, it was in the talking newsreels of the 1930s that both he and Neville Chamberlain surpassed their opponents. In a typical performance, in 1936, Baldwin was pictured apparently at his desk in 10 Downing Street, taking stock of the world and finding Britain best, because Britain had adopted the sensible path of coalition and so avoided the horrors of civil confrontation. In fact, he was not in 10 Downing Street at all, but in a set built by Conservative Central Office which the newsreel company had agreed to use. [DOCUMENT XVI] Chamberlain was the first Chancellor of the Exchequer to use the newsreels to explain his annual budget. His performances were increasingly assured, and it is clear that the Conservatives had found an outlet in mass communication rather more loyal than the press barons. This was to culminate in the ecstatic reception given to Chamberlain by the newsreels at the time of the Munich agreement, in which he was described as showing 'the common sense of the man in the street'. [DOCUMENT II] This was, in a real sense, the high point of success of Baldwin's populist strategy for inter-war conservatism. 'Posterity will thank God, as we do now, that in our time of desperate need, our safety was guarded by such a man – Neville Chamberlain.'

MacDonald and Labour

Labour's emergence as a major political party was nowhere near as easy as the pessimists in the Conservative party had expected. The 1918 constitution confirmed the alliance between the Trades Union Congress and the party, though it also put added emphasis on the constituency parties and the need to build a political machine outside industry. Clause IV of the constitution committed the party, in rather vague terms, to the collective ownership of the means of production, but the emphasis was on Labour's evolutionary road to socialism through democracy. Indeed Labour was, if anything, even more anxious to distance itself from the extreme left than from the traditional parliamentary parties. Not only did Labour reject the application for affiliation by the Communist party, but it also denied individual membership to anyone belonging to the CP. Labour also refused to work with communist-inspired groups like the Minority Movement or the National Unemployed Workers Movement to deal with the problems of the socially deprived. In the same way, in the 1930s, Labour rejected out of hand the idea of sharing a platform with the extreme left in its condemnation of Fascism and appeasement.

Labour's electoral position was problematic while the Liberal party refused to die. Although the Liberals had been split in 1918, the combined vote of the splintered groups could still effectively deny Labour the chance of government for most of the 1920s. Labour won 22 per cent of the popular vote in 1918 but only 1 per cent more than the combined Liberal vote in 1923, when it came to power in a minority government for the first time. In 1929, again, Labour could not attain an overall majority. Three-party politics was a genuine factor in the elections of the twenties, in other words, and the working class, newly dominant in the electorate, did not switch automatically *en masse* to Labour. Baldwinism undoubtedly did make some inroads into what should have been in-the-bank Labour support, but the refusal of some skilled workers to give up their traditional Liberal vote was also a factor. Studies seem to suggest, too, that the franchise for women favoured the Conservatives. Indeed, the complete collapse of the Labour vote in 1931 made it unclear whether Labour would ever be able to achieve an overall majority over the other parties. The crucial factor, however, was the electoral geography produced by the depression. While the vast bulk of the electorate, centred in the south and Midlands of England, was not unemployed, not badly housed and not relatively deprived, Labour could not hope to win an election simply on the backs of the unemployed. Although the party began to pile up huge majorities in the depressed areas, they were simply outgunned by the Conservatives in the shires and in suburbia. In effect, the percentage of the popular vote they did obtain was skewed; it was not well distributed nationally. What this meant was that Labour had to try to appeal to the same constituency as the Conservatives, to those who were doing relatively well in the depression years. Ramsay MacDonald's strategy of projecting Labour as a 'respectable alternative' to Toryism was the only practical policy for a party that had specifically rejected the revolutionary approach and was committed to socialism through the ballot box.

Nowhere was this more apparent than in Labour's financial policy. Philip Snowden, Labour's spokesman on economic affairs, and Chancellor of the Exchequer in 1924 and from 1929 to 1931, was purely orthodox in his view that the role of the Chancellor was to resist public expenditure until it could not be resisted, and then to limit the sums to the minimum possible. In 1924, Labour dropped the idea of a levy on capital to reduce the National Debt and offered major Cabinet posts to former Liberals, mostly peers, partly in an attempt to attract support from the Liberal party and partly to gain a Labour presence in the House of Lords. Snowden dropped the import levies which had been imposed by the former Conservative administration and produced a classic free-trade budget. It was clear that, relying on the support of Asquith and the Liberals for majorities in the Commons, the government could not last long. But MacDonald had put Liberals in an acute tactical bind and, in the election of December 1924, though seats were lost, Labour increased its share of the popular vote by over one million on 1923. The Liberals, on the other hand, were reduced to just forty seats, and were virtually wiped out in England. Even then, they had recovered sufficiently by 1929 once again to deny Labour an overall majority.

After 1924, Labour continued to project extremely orthodox financial policies. Churchill was criticized as Chancellor for not cutting public expenditure more fully, and for not contributing more to the Sinking Fund to reduce the National Debt. There was always the danger, of course, that the policy of the respectable alternative would attract middle-of-the-road voters but annoy the left wing of the Labour party. When Labour came back to power in 1929, again reliant on Liberal support in the Commons, the left began a more vociferous attack on the Labour leadership. With unemployment spiralling upwards after the Wall Street crash, Sir Oswald Mosley called for a programme of direct state intervention in 1930, including nationalization of industry, counter-cyclical investment and the imposition of tariffs. Snowden rejected the proposals outright. Mosley soon left the party and stampeded on a bizarre political path that finally led to his formation of the British Union of Fascists. Snowden also rejected similar proposals from the group which considered itself to be the ideological soul of Labour, the Independent Labour Party. The leadership could therefore expect little sympathy from the left when the crisis hit in 1931. In a minority position in Parliament, the government was unable to resist opposition demands for a full inquiry into the effect of the increased costs of unemployment on public spending and on international confidence. When the subsequent May report forecast a budgetary deficit of £120 million for 1932, and a deficit of £105 million on the Unemployment Insurance Fund, the run on gold in the Bank of England became critical. The government wrestled as best it could with a situation it simply could not control, partly because of the after-effects of the Wall Street crash, partly because of its financial orthodoxy, but mostly because of its minority position. While the Cabinet agreed substantial cuts in public expenditure, they could not agree cuts in unemployment benefit. Although further pressure from the opposition forced the government to think again, MacDonald could only secure Cabinet agreement by a small majority. The left assumed he would resign. They were astounded when he resigned as prime minister of a Labour government and immediately assumed the leadership of a coalition, excluding all those who had opposed him in cabinet.

The ensuing general election was a rout for Labour, which was reduced to just fifty seats in the House of Commons. The later myth of the 'great betrayal' of 1931 laid the blame for the disaster firmly on the shoulders of MacDonald and Snowden. Both of them were expelled from the Labour party, while Snowden accused his former colleagues of 'running away' from a crisis. This was the point. The strategy of the respectable alternative demanded that Labour deal with the realities of power in a crisis of capitalism, and not simply resign, walk away and leave it to the opposition to do what there was no alternative to doing. [**DOCUMENT XVII**] Although MacDonald was now a prisoner of the Conservatives in electoral terms, and increasingly isolated in Cabinet after Neville Chamberlain took over the Exchequer from Snowden, he still saw himself as carrying the Labour flag: 'they can take the label from my back', he insisted, 'but they cannot take it from my soul.' Labour was forced back on its bedrock support in the depressed areas in 1931. Here, their vote remained solid, even increased. Indeed, they still retained almost exactly the same percentage of the popular vote as they had achieved in December 1923, when they had actually come to power. The problem was that 30.5 per cent of the vote in 1923 produced 191 seats, while 30.7 per cent in 1931 produced only fifty-two. Their vote had collapsed in the relatively prosperous areas where it was essential to win if Labour were to form a government.

For the rest of the thirties, the Labour opposition was led by the ineffectual pacifist, George Lansbury, and then by Clement Attlee, who was later to be a great prime minister but was never a leader with charisma. In an age when mass communications were coming to dominate politics, only Ramsay MacDonald had been able to compare with Baldwin and Chamberlain in terms of public projection of personality and policies. Although Labour did regain some of the ground lost in 1931 in the general election of 1935, there are no reasons for believing that Labour could have returned to power in 1940, when the next election was due. They won in 1945 because of the interposition of the Second World War. Yet the 'great betrayal' of 1931 had two paradoxical benefits for Labour in the longer term. First, it meant that the party could retain control of the left in the nation as a whole. There were to be no catastrophic desertions of support to the Communists. The rump of the party after 1931 could claim that the alternative economic strategy put forward by the left had never been tried, that it was MacDonald and Snowden who had failed, not Labour. Second, it meant that Labour could not be held responsible for the failures in foreign policy which were to ensue from the massive majorities enjoyed by the National Governments in the 1930s. Labour could claim, indeed, that the 'great betrayal' had doomed the unemployed to the means test and doomed the nation to another war.

Appeasement

It is unlikely that any serious politician in Britain thought that the international settlement at the end of the First World War could be sustained indefinitely. What was attained in the peace treaties was simply the best compromise that could be obtained between competing demands. The French might well have been prepared to accept a less stringent peace if the Americans or the British had been prepared to guarantee France's frontiers. As the Americans began to return to isolation, however, the British would not give such a guarantee on their own. The situation in eastern Europe was also very disturbing, with the collapse of Austria-Hungary and the Russian Empire. The ever-predictably reactionary Romanovs had been replaced by a very unpredictable Communist government, which might or might not be bent on world revolution. A whole range of competing nationalities had emerged in place of the Austro-Hungarian

Dual Monarchy, but the demands for national self-determination were difficult to meet when ethnic distribution did not always match frontiers that made strategic or economic sense. In the event, it seemed that every people's demand for national self-determination had been largely met except that of the Germans.

It was reasonable enough to assume, on the other hand, that time would provide opportunities for adjustments to the settlement. The British hoped that, as the war faded into the past, the French would come to be more sympathetic and that Germany could be brought back into the comity of nations. The League of Nations they saw as an opportunity for negotiation and appeasement of both French and German grievances. It was important for Britain that Germany should be allowed to recover great-nation status as soon as possible, not only because a weak Germany added instability in central Europe to that in eastern Europe, but for economic reasons. It was clear that British economic recovery depended on European economic recovery, and European economic recovery in turn depended on a Germany which was both economically and politically stable. Weimar governments were threatened from both the political right and the left in the 1920s, but Gustav Streseman did at least have some success in negotiating with the erstwhile victors. The cycle of reparation payments, war debts and American loans kept Germany artificially weak, however, and set up the Weimar Republic for a testing time after the Wall Street crash, culminating in Hitler's coming to power early in 1933. It was one of the misfortunes that faced British diplomats in the 1930s that the obvious weaknesses and injustices of the post-war settlement could not be negotiated away before the depression changed the political face of Germany. Nevertheless, it was still clear that Germany was unjustly treated at Versailles, and those injustices did not become any less obvious just because they were articulated by someone as politically ugly as Adolf Hitler. It could, in a sense, be argued that Hitler himself was partly a result of Versailles, and that concession might undermine his *raison d'être*.

Britain, anyway, had never considered herself simply a European power. Her interest in Europe was to maintain a balance of power which would prevent any single nation dominating the Continent. In the situation after the First World War, there was no balance of power at all because of the instability of central and eastern Europe. A new balance had to be built. Britain was just as concerned with her role as a world power, with an Empire now larger than ever through her League of Nations mandates. In the Far East, a new power had emerged. The Anglo-Japanese alliance of 1902 had been Britain's way of attempting to build a balance in the Far East. The alliance had been the first major international recognition of Japan and had the effect of buttressing Japan against Russia in the area. With the collapse of Russia, however, the Americans were increasingly convinced that the Anglo-Japanese alliance was bolstering those militant Japanese interests with designs on the Pacific Rim and beyond. At the Washington conference, in 1922, the Americans demanded, in return for an agreement to limit their capital ships to the same number as Britain, that the Anglo-Japanese alliance be allowed to lapse. This seemed naive to the British, and perhaps a cover for America's own ambitions in the area, but they had no choice but to concede. Once again isolated, and facing their own economic problems, the influence of the militants in Japan increased. It should be remembered that the first major military threat to the post-war *status quo* happened not in Europe but in China. The British decision to consider rearmament was taken not because of some future threat from Germany, but because of the immediate threat posed to British possessions in the Far East by Japan, in the wake of her invasion of Manchuria in 1931.

In 1935, Mussolini's invasion of Abyssinia found Britain having to support the League of Nations when it was clearly not in her national interest to do so. Having a hostile power athwart the major route of imperial communication, the Mediterranean, was a serious matter. But the pact that the British foreign secretary, Sir Samuel Hoare, tried to fix with his French opposite number, Pierre Laval, would have sold out Abyssinia and undermined the League of Nations. The demise of the Hoare–Laval plan, under pressure of public opinion, left both the British and the French with the worst of all worlds. The League had been fatally weakened and would never again be seriously invoked. Mussolini got Abyssinia anyway, and now regarded Britain and France as hostile, which drove him into liaison with Hitler. This was in spite of Italo-German differences over Austria, which the British and French had hoped to exploit to keep the two Fascist leaders apart. By 1936, then, the situation was that Britain faced three potentially hostile powers. While it might be possible to defeat each of these powers separately, if it came to war, the prospect of fighting all three powers simultaneously was daunting. This was particularly true when it was not at all clear that the Americans would fight to save the British Empire, and the Soviets would certainly not do so.

Neville Chamberlain, when he moved from the Exchequer to the premiership in 1937 on Baldwin's retirement, brought with him the 'Treasury mentality'. The Treasury limited money to be made available for rearmament because it thought that it threatened economic recovery. Even so, Britain was spending more on defence in peacetime by 1939 than she had ever spent before. Yet it is doubtful whether Britain could have mounted a serious deterrent to a war on three fronts. The Royal Navy, for example, reckoned that it needed no fewer than seventy extra cruisers to deal with a three-front war. By way of contrast, before the First World War, government had blanched at the demand for only eight dreadnoughts. On top of that, new weaponry created new defence demands. Air power threatened to leap over Britain's traditional protection, the Channel, and the air theorists claimed that mass air attack would destroy cities and panic civilian populations into demands for peace, or even into revolutionary action. To British governments which spent the depression trying to offset the prospect of social conflict, the threat of air power to the fabric of the country seemed real enough. Baldwin had summed up the mood when he had warned in 1932 that 'the bomber will always get through', and that the result would be huge civilian casualties if an air war ever occurred. Even in early 1940, the Cabinet office was reckoning on the possibility of 60,000 fatalities in every day of sustained air attack. It is certainly not clear how long any civilian population could have coped with that degree of slaughter. In fact, Britain only suffered marginally more than 60,000 fatalities from bombing over the whole of the war, but these were the official estimates which so frightened the politicians and the public in the 1930s.

Chamberlain's response to this complex of problems when he became prime minister was to concentrate on its German aspect. Germany possessed the only air force capable of attacking Britain. The appeasement of Germany would automatically solve the other international problems, because Italy and Japan would never dare cut loose on their own. If Germany were not appeased, however, the result would be a three-front war which might well see the home country flattened by air attack and the Empire lost to the Italians and the Japanese. Why would Britain risk this for Czechoslovakia which was, as the prime minister remarked, 'a faraway country of which we know nothing'? The Sudeten Germans themselves wanted to be included in Greater Germany. The Sudetenland had only been included in the new Czechoslovak state after the war because it made a more sensible frontier. As the British ambassador in Berlin warned, the Germans were prepared to fight for it. Since Britain had no immediate method of intervening to save Czechoslovakia from invasion, a long war would result. Even if Britain won that war, Sir Nevile Henderson pointed out, there was little likelihood that Britain would recreate Czechoslovakia in its current form and start the problem all over again. The chiefs of staff warned that, until the number of potential enemies had been reduced, Britain should only fight for what was absolutely vital to her own interests. [DOCUMENT XVIII] It would be an unusual prime minister to decide on war when all the professional advice was that the cause was wrong and the outcome doubtful.

Where Chamberlain was vulnerable was in the way that he personalized the policy of appeasement. While his approach to the problem of the three-front war was logical enough, he was no expert in the field of world affairs and lacked understanding of the manifold ways in which diplomatic pressure can be brought to bear. He managed to weaken rather than maintain a front of friendly powers, for instance, and proffered deals which were one-sided rather than mutually beneficial. Chamberlain's decision to take over diplomacy personally suggested that he felt himself to have something that career diplomats lacked. What he gave Hitler in signing the Munich treaty, and being photographed with the dictators just after the event, was a hint of personal approval. Even more, there was a hint that this was a triumph for right-minded values, rather than a pragmatic deal struck to avoid something worse. The crusading zeal of his shuttle diplomacy in 1938 also created public expectation and celebration of a lasting peace which even Chamberlain himself perhaps did not believe. The razzmatazz of Munich only made the eventual failure of appeasement, and the personal failure of Chamberlain, all the more public and transparent. [DOCUMENTS I and II]

Inter-war becomes history: 1940

While the ascendancy of Baldwin and Chamberlain was assured by 1931, there emerged among younger members of the Conservative party, as well as in the Labour party, the seeds of a new cross-party commitment to wider state intervention. In organizations like Political and Economic Planning, the Next Five Years Group and the League of Nations Union, younger Conservatives such as Harold

Macmillan rubbed shoulders with Labour and Liberal supporters and developed broadly similar ideas about the possible value of state planning for organized growth. They were educated in the ideas of John Maynard Keynes, and considered the prospects for international organizations that might approach more successfully than national governments the economic and political issues that had beset the world since 1918. Important for the future as this 'middle opinion' may have been in the 1930s, it stood no chance of reaching fruition until the politically dominant views of the 1930s had been fundamentally challenged by the outbreak and the first year of the Second World War.

The challenge came from an unlikely source. If Churchill was 'in the wilderness' in the 1930s, he largely had himself to blame. Never known for his party loyalty, his split with the leadership over the possibility of relaxing the British hold on India cost him the chance of further posts in a Cabinet headed by Baldwin. His stance against appeasement was often intemperate, illogical and factually flawed. Critics felt, too, that it ill became the man who had been Chancellor in the 1920s, and who had overseen large cuts in defence, to complain once it proved difficult to reverse those cuts in the 1930s. In spite of his magisterial thundering against the Munich agreement, he did not seem to try to cultivate any personal following in the Commons. Nevertheless, by 1939 he was the only leading Conservative who had been wholly unequivocal in his attitude to Nazi Germany. On top of that, the fact that no one had more experience than he in the practical or political side of defence, meant that he could not be excluded from the Cabinet when war was declared. Chamberlain, meanwhile, had committed a series of devastating political mistakes in the first six months of the war. He had admitted publicly on the day war was declared that everything he had fought for in public life was crashing in ruins about him, hardly the rallying call the nation needed, and then, lulled by the 'phoney war' after the quick defeat of Poland, he declared that Hitler had 'missed the bus'. The subsequent invasion of Scandinavia by Germany, pre-empting a badly co-ordinated series of British moves to mine Scandinavian waters, sealed his fate. On 1 September 1939, when Chamberlain had hesitated after the German invasion of Poland, Arthur Greenwood rose to reply for Labour. As he did so, the right-wing Conservative Leo Amery had shouted across the chamber of the House of Commons, 'Speak for England, Arthur!' This was perhaps the first clear indication that the right in the

Conservative party might be able to align itself in an unholy alliance with Labour to defeat the centrist politics of Baldwin and Chamberlain that had dominated for so long. In May 1940, as Chamberlain tried to rally Conservative support after the Norway fiasco, Amery demanded of Chamberlain, as Oliver Cromwell had demanded of the Long Parliament, 'In the name of God, go!' Chamberlain was reluctant to do that, and it says something for the sheer strength of the Conservative party that, in the vote of confidence that followed, he still had a majority of over eighty. Nevertheless, his majority was so much less than expected that it was clear that the National Government would have to be reformed. Labour refused to serve in a government led by Chamberlain. Lord Halifax, foreign secretary and the obvious successor, felt that his position in the House of Lords would make the premiership impossible to sustain in a total war in an age of mass democracy. The leadership fell, virtually by default, to Churchill. Churchill, feeling that he was 'walking with destiny', immediately offered the deputy premiership to Clement Attlee, and all the most important posts on the home front to Labour. He even moved to find a parliamentary seat for one of his most fearsome opponents in the General Strike fourteen years previously, the general secretary of the Transport and General Workers' Union, Ernest Bevin, who became minister of labour.

Churchill became the warlord, but the home front was to be dominated by Labour. Besides Attlee and Bevin, Herbert Morrison became home secretary. Also to the Home Office as minister of state came Ellen Wilkinson, 'Red Ellen' as she was known in the thirties, who had been told by Walter Runciman, President of the Board of Trade back in the 1920s, that the town she represented, Jarrow, 'must seek its own salvation'. A succession of important jobs went to Stafford Cripps, the left-wing bugbear of inter-war conservatism. Churchill was either unwilling or unable to give a lead to the Conservatives at home, who drifted between, on the one hand, the traditionalist views of groups like Aims of Industry and, on the other hand, the way of thinking which had emerged from the 'middle opinion' of the 1930s and which crystallized into the Tory Reform Group in 1943. The Second World War seemed to prove what the First had implied, that state intervention worked in wartime. The experience of the inter-war years now raised the question of why state intervention should not work in peacetime. Why should not the warfare state become the welfare state? Fundamentally, however, it was the cultural underpinning of the reformed coalition that gave it its longer-term implications. In 1940 the great proletarian novel of the 1930s, *Love on the Dole*, was finally filmed, and the inter-war years were recontextualized as the time of despair before the years of ambition, the years of a people's war. Almost ten years after the novel appeared, in an optimistic rewriting of an originally starkly pessimistic text, *Love on the Dole* looked forward to the catastrophe of war, which would create the opportunity for a new Britain:

> Millions of men in this country want work. Millions of men in other countries are in the same boat too . . . You can think of it as a kind of big dam that's already beginning to crack. And next year, or the year after, or maybe in ten years, there'll be a catastrophe. You see, that's the way of the world and nature. It takes a disaster for people to realise. But life goes on. What we've got to remember is that human conditions are not beyond human control. I said that man has made these conditions. Well he can remake them! And build a new and better world.

By 1945, such views of the thirties, and of what the experience of the subsequent war meant in relation to those years, had become commonplace. The Conservatives had become the 'guilty men'. At the end of the war, Labour was swept to power in a landslide election victory. Over the next six years, they put into place the welfare state. They also took the decision to build the atomic bomb which, they assumed, would mean that they would never have to appease the Soviets. The shock of defeat for the Conservatives in 1945 was enough to bring the Tory Reformers to the forefront of the party and, when the Conservatives returned to power in 1951, most of the legislation that Labour had put in place since the war was to prove safe with them. From then until the mid-1970s, there was a broadly shared belief that the welfare state at home, with the Cold War abroad, was the right way to run the country.

This was the political legacy of the inter-war years. But when Michael Foot, one of the men who had written *Guilty Men* in the first place, came to lead the Labour party in the early 1980s, the myths had faded. Thatcherism attacked the shibboleths of post-1945 orthodoxy, once again withdrawing the state from the interventionist role it had taken in response to the reaction to the years of depression. Once again democracy in Britain appeared to prefer the Conservatives, even in a depression, and once more Labour looked marginalized. In fact, it was only when Labour forgot the thirties that the party was to look electable again. Once again the general assumption was that the state should not intervene rather than that it should. The years between the wars played a pivotal role in shaping late twentieth-century Britain. It was in those years that Britain began to deal with the problems of relative economic decline, began nevertheless to enjoy an unprecedented rise in the standard of living, became conscious of relative deprivation, began to have traffic problems, began to live in huge suburbs that looked the same whatever the city, began to share a cross-class popular culture. The period no longer reeks, however, of the political myths that dominated in the three decades after 1940. In this sense, the inter-war years have finally become history.

Tables

Table 1 Production

Looking at the quarterly index of production allows us to see not just which years were good and bad ones, but which times of the year were likely to be better for trade and therefore for employment. Because of the considerable changes in prices after the First World War, figures of value of production tend to be rather misleading: much more useful comparison is produced by converting figures to constant prices. In these statistics, all figures have been converted to 1924 prices. They are based on figures produced in the monthly publication, The London and Cambridge Economic Service Bulletin.

Quarterly index of production, seasonally adjusted (1924 average = 100)

	Mar.	June	Sept.	Dec.
1920	116	117	120	102
1921	86	56	90	84
1922	83	90	99	91
1923	95	100	96	100
1924	95	102	102	101
1925	99	100	94	97
1926	98	74	60	68
1927	107	111	110	105
1928	102	106	99	103
1929	104	114	113	112
1930	106	.103	94	90
1931	82	82	84	88
1932	88	85	81	85
1933	85	91	92	95

	Mar.	June	Sept.	Dec.
1934	99	105	101	103
1935	100	111	109	114
1936	112	121	119	119
1937	115	129	126	125
1938	118	111	103	106

(F. Capie and M. Collins, *The Inter-War British Economy: A Statistical Abstract* (Manchester, Manchester University Press, 1983), p.20)

Table 2 House-building

The inter-war years proved to be unusually productive in house-building after the unusually unproductive decade during which the Great War occurred. It was also a period in which central government and local government action made a substantial difference to the figures.

1. Additions to the housing stock, 1861–1939

Decade ending	Percentage addition to stock
1861	14.3
1871	15.2
1881	15.4
1891	11.6
1901	15.2
1911	12.5
1921	3.7
1931	17.8
1939*	25.0

*The 1939 figure is for the years 1931–9.

(General Register Office, *Census of England and Wales, 1931, Housing Report*, p.x; M. Bowley, *Housing and the State* (1945), appendix 2, reprinted in S. Glynn and J. Oxborrow, *Interwar Britain: A Social and Economic History* (London, George Allen and Unwin, 1976), p.227)

2. Private and local authority building, 1919–1939

	England and Wales	Scotland
Built by local authorities	1, 112, 505	212, 866
Built by private enterprise with subsidy	430, 327	43, 067
Built by private enterprise without subsidy	2, 449, 216	61, 444
	3, 992, 048	317, 377
Total: Great Britain	4,309,425	

(From Royal Commission on the Distribution of the Industrial Population, 1940; reprinted in Glynn and Oxborrow, *Interwar Britain: A Social and Economic History*, p.67)

Table 3 The cost of living

The Ministry of Labour began an official Cost of Living Index at the beginning of the First World War. Clearly, in a total war, there was important political information to be gathered about the everyday expenditure of the working class: it could be used in relation to negotiations with trade unions over wages, for example, and also to gauge the likely impact of taxation increases. The index covered the cost of food, rent, clothing, fuel and light, and of other significant expenditure such as newspapers, bus and railway fares and cigarettes. Although published monthly in the Ministry of Labour Gazette, *variations from month to month were not wild, so only the figures for three months of each year have been reproduced here. To ensure comparability, the figures are in constant 1924 prices.*

Ministry of Labour, Cost of Living Index, seasonally adjusted (1924 average = 100)

	Mar.	June	Sept.	Dec.
1919	122	120	124	127
1920	135	146	149	149
1921	135	127	119	108
1922	106	106	101	100
1923	101	98	99	100
1924	101	98	99	101
1925	102	100	99	99
1926	97	98	99	98
1927	96	96	95	94
1928	95	95	94	94
1929	94	93	94	94
1930	91	89	88	86
1931	85	85	82	83
1932	84	82	81	80
1933	80	79	80	80
1934	81	81	81	81
1935	81	82	82	83
1936	84	84	84	86
1937	88	89	89	90
1938	89	91	88	88
1939	89	89	94	98

(Abstracted from Capie and Collins, *The Inter-War British Economy: A Statistical Abstract*, p.38)

Table 4 Wages

Figures on average weekly wages were compiled by A. L. Bowley for the London and Cambridge Economic Service, and were based on the average weekly wage rates of twenty skilled and unskilled occupational groups, weighted according to the 1924 Census of Production. The groups were specifically chosen to include representatives of time rates and piece rates, skilled and unskilled workers, as well as male and female workers. Note that these figures are weekly wage rates, not earnings, and take no account of overtime. The LCES compiled figures monthly. Listed below are the comparative figures for four months of each year from 1925 to 1939. For comparability, figures are given at constant 1924 prices.

Index of average weekly wages (1924 average = 100)

	Mar.	June	Sept.	Dec.
1925	100.8	100.5	100.5	100.5
1926	100.5	100.5	100.5	101.5
1927	101.0	100.5	100.8	100.5
1928	99.7	99.7	99.5	99.5
1929	99.5	99.5	99.0	99.0
1930	98.5	98.2	98.2	98.2
1931	97.5	97.0	96.8	96.5
1932	95.5	95.5	95.2	94.5
1933	94.0	94.0	94.0	94.0
1934	94.0	94.0	94.0	94.2
1935	94.2	94.7	95.7	95.7
1936	97.0	97.2	98.0	98.0
1937	100.0	100.7	101.7	103.0
1938	104.0	104.5	104.5	104.5
1939	105.0	105.8	106.0	109.2

(Abstracted from Capie and Collins, *The Inter-War British Economy: A Statistical Abstract*, p.62)

Table 5 Wholesale prices

The Board of Trade took a large number of commodities to draw up their monthly index of wholesale prices. This included raw materials, semi-finished articles sold on for finishing, as well as fully finished articles. These commodities were also weighted according to their relative value established in the Census of Production. Four of the monthly figures for each of the inter-war years are listed. They show a drop in wholesale prices even more spectacular than the drop in the cost of living. For comparability, figures are shown at constant 1924 prices.

Board of Trade, Wholesale Price Index, seasonally adjusted (1924 average = 100)

	Mar.	June	Sept.	Dec.
1919	153	144	159	177
1920	193	194	186	158
1921	128	120	112	100
1922	97	97	92	93
1923	97	96	95	98
1924	100	98	100	102
1925	101	95	93	91
1926	87	88	91	88
1927	85	86	85	84
1928	85	87	83	83
1929	85	82	82	79
1930	75	73	69	65
1931	64	63	60	63
1932	63	59	61	61
1933	59	61	62	62
1934	64	63	63	63
1935	63	64	64	66
1936	66	67	69	72
1937	78	80	80	77
1938	75	73	70	71
1939	70	71	76	87

(Abstracted from Capie and Collins, *The Inter-War British Economy: A Statistical Abstract*, p.32)

Table 6 Unemployment

The main source for deriving figures of unemployment for the inter-war years is the operation of the National Insurance Act. After 1920, when national insurance was extended to cover the majority of the work-force, whether manual or non-manual, these figures must be pretty reliable. They include as unemployed those on short-time work who qualified for benefit under the insurance scheme, as well as those at government training centres. Those under sixteen years of age are not included, however, and the figures for the period after 1931 may be affected by the large number of married women excluded from claiming benefit by new regulations in that year.

Ministry of Labour, Percentage of Insured Workers Unemployed (seasonally adjusted)

	Mar.	June	Sept.	Dec.
1920	3.4	2.5	4.0	7.8
1921	14.7	21.6	15.1	17.7
1922	15.3	13.2	13.5	12.6
1923	11.2	10.9	12.5	10.4
1924	9.4	9.0	11.3	10.5
1925	10.6	11.5	12.8	10.2
1926	10.4	14.6	13.5	12.0
1927	10.4	8.8	9.2	9.9
1928	10.1	10.7	11.2	11.2
1929	10.6	9.6	9.8	11.1
1930	14.5	15.4	17.3	20.1
1931	22.2	21.2	22.1	20.9
1932	22.0	22.2	22.5	21.8
1933	21.1	20.2	19.2	17.5
1934	16.6	17.1	16.7	16.0
1935	15.8	16.1	15.6	14.1
1936	13.7	13.4	12.6	12.0
1937	11.2	10.4	10.1	12.1
1938	12.3	13.8	13.4	12.9
1939	11.8	10.0	9.5	9.1

(Abstracted from Capie and Collins, *The Inter-War British Economy: A Statistical Abstract*, p.63)

Illustrative Documents

DOCUMENT I Contemporary judgements: *Guilty Men*

In the summer of 1940, as Churchill replaced Chamberlain as prime minister and the Germans swept through Scandinavia, the Low Countries and France, three journalists wrote the first and the most famous denunciation of appeasement and the appeasers. Michael Foot, Peter Howard and Frank Owen worked for Beaverbrook newspapers. Foot was to go on to become a leading light on the left wing of the Labour party and to become party leader during the bitter struggles of the early 1980s. Guilty Men *was published by Gollancz Press, in the same format as Gollancz's famous Left Book Club editions of the 1930s. It was advertised as* Victory Books No. 1 *and sold massively over the next couple of years. It was presented as a kind of play or, perhaps, a parody, and each chapter had a cast. The first chapter featured the doomed army at Dunkirk, described at the end of the chapter as 'an army doomed before they took the field'. Subsequent chapters traced the story of what brought about the disaster.*

When Mr Chamberlain stepped out of his airplane on the return from Munich, he had said, 'This means Peace in our Time'.

After he got back to Downing Street he shouted from the window, 'I bring you Peace with honour'. He also remarked, 'Out of this nettle, danger, we pluck this flower, safety'.

Nobody can accuse Mr Chamberlain of being a wilful liar. He said those things because he believed them. He was absolutely satisfied that when Hitler signed that little piece of paper, the heart of a man who had built up his regime of treachery, lies and deception had changed.

At a dinner party shortly after Munich, the British Prime Minister found himself sitting near to a politician who had opposed the settlement. A discussion arose between the two men and was conducted in most friendly terms.

The Premier's opponent asked how any trust could reasonably be placed in Hitler's word. He pointed out that as long ago as 1933 Hitler said in the Reichstag, 'The German people have no thought of invading any other country'. In 1934 he said, 'After the Saar question is settled, the German government is ready to accept not only the letter but also the spirit of the Locarno Pact'. In May 1935, in the Reichstag, the German Fuhrer said, 'Germany neither intends nor wishes to interfere in the internal affairs of Austria, to annex Austria or to conclude an Anschluss'. In March 1936 he affirmed, 'We have no territorial demands in Europe'.

In February 1938 he reaffirmed his recognition of Austrian sovereignty already expressed in the Austro-German agreement of July 1936.

In March 1938 he gave assurances that Germany had no hostile intention against Czechoslovakia.

Having recited all these broken pledges, this fellow guest turned towards Mr Chamberlain at the dinner table and asked, 'Prime Minister, in the face of all this, remembering all these things, do you not feel a twinge of doubt about Hitler's promises?'

Mr Chamberlain replied with complete gravity, 'Ah, but this time he promised *me* . . .'

(Cato, *Guilty Men* (London, Gollancz, 1940), pp.59–60.)

DOCUMENT II The four-power conference

The Conservatives', and particularly Chamberlain's, careful grooming of the newsreel companies culminated in the heroic reception they gave the prime minister at the climax of appeasement with the Munich agreement. Gaumont British released a special issue on the Four Power Conference which began with footage of the signing of the agreement, switched to a potted history of the troubles in Asia and Europe since Versailles, and culminated with Chamberlain's return to Heston aerodrome. The implication was that the prime minister had finally succeeded where a generation of diplomats had failed. The cameras concentrated on Chamberlain as he read the famous declaration, and then followed his group's cars through packed streets to Buckingham Palace. In the last frames the prime minister was pictured on the balcony of Buckingham Palace with the King and Queen.

Commentary over: So the Prime Minister has come back from this third and greatest journey, and he said . . .

Chamberlain: that the settlement of the Czechoslovak problem which has now been achieved is, in my view, only the prelude to a larger settlement in which all of Europe may find peace. [*Cheers*] This morning I had another talk with the German Chancellor, Herr Hitler, and here is the paper which bears his name upon it as well as mine. [*Holds paper aloft. Cheers from the crowd*] Some of you have perhaps already heard what it contains, but I would just like to read it to you:

> We, the German Fuehrer and Chancellor and the British Prime Minister, have had a further meeting today and are agreed in recognizing that the question of Anglo-German relations is of the first importance for the two countries and for Europe. We regard the agreement signed last night and the Anglo-German Naval Agreement as symbolic of the desire of our two peoples never to go to war with one another again. [*Cheers*] We are resolved that the method of consultation [*Hear! Hear!*] shall be the method adopted to deal with any other question that may concern our two countries and we are determined to continue our efforts to remove possible sources of difference, and thus to contribute to the surer peace of Europe. [*Loud cheers*]

Commentary over: There was no sign of British reserve as the crowds fought to get near the premier's car. [*Cheers*]

As we travelled back with Mr Chamberlain from Heston we drove through serried masses of happy people, happy in the knowledge that there was no war with Germany. [*Land of Hope and Glory*, begins quietly in the background, mingling with the cheers]

The premier drove straight to Buckingham Palace. Here he was received by the King while London waited. And history was made again when Their Majesties came out on to the famous balcony with the prime minister. [*Land of Hope and Glory*, reaches its climax, now at same volume as cheering]

Posterity will thank God, as we do now, that in our time of desperate need, our safety was guarded by such a man – Neville Chamberlain!

('The four power conference', *Gaumont British News*, 3 October 1938, reproduced on InterUniversity History Film Consortium videocassette, *Neville Chamberlain.*)

DOCUMENT III Poverty, 1899 and 1936

S. B. Rowntree, a member of the Quaker chocolate-making family, undertook three surveys of the condition of the working class in his native York, the first in 1899, the second in 1936 and the third in 1951. Together they constitute an absorbing picture of the life of the worst-off sections of society. Although Rowntree is often quoted as providing damning evidence of social conditions in inter-war Britain, he was in fact quite clear that a great deal had actually improved since his first survey. Note, for example, his argument that the comparison between 1899 and 1936 would have favoured the latter even more, had it not been for the fact that 1936 happened to be an unusually bad year for unemployment in York. His point was that the British should not be complacent about the advances made. Note also his concern that the lower birth rate might make people more prosperous but might also threaten the future of the race. The publication of Poverty and Progress *in wartime – particularly the People's War year of 1940 – altered entirely the context of its reception and made it a primer for post-war reconstruction.*

I suggest that we should probably not be very far wrong if we put the standard of living available to the workers in 1936 at about 36 per cent higher than it was in 1899.

Three reasons account for this increase. The first is the reduction in the size of family . . . we cannot say exactly what part it plays, but it has certainly played an important part in raising the standard of comfort attainable by the workers. The fact that there has been a substantial increase in the family income is a matter for unqualified satisfaction, but the fall in the birth rate from 30 per thousand in 1899 to 15 per thousand in 1936 is regarded by many as a matter of grave concern.

The second reason accounting for the improvement which has occurred in the standard of comfort available to the workers is the increase in real wages, probably amounting on the average to about 35 per cent. The effect of this upon the average per capita income would have been greater but for the heavy unemployment in 1936.

A third cause is the remarkable growth of social services during the period under review. In 1899 the only financial aid given from public sources to persons living in their homes was Poor Relief, the acceptance of which rendered the recipients paupers; they lost their rights as citizens, for they could not vote. Almost universally pauperism was regarded as a stigma which self-respecting persons would avoid if at all possible. Many a family preferred to starve rather than to ask for Poor Relief.

(S. B. Rowntree, *Poverty and Progress* (London, Longmans, 1940), pp. 453–4.)

DOCUMENT IV The causes of poverty

It was calculated by Rowntree that 6.8 per cent of the working class in York were living in primary poverty (which he defined as subsistence level, the standard of income below which physical deterioration set in) as opposed to 15.46 per cent in 1899. Had it not been for heavy unemployment in 1936, primary poverty would have been very much lower. For 1936, however, he felt that the standard applied in 1899 was far too stringent as a poverty line. He adopted instead a standard which allowed a frugal family to buy not only sufficient food, clothing, heating and lighting, as well as having a little left over to pay for insurance, transport and newspapers, but also enough to pay for a radio licence, holidays, cinema, beer and tobacco. Of the working class, he calculated that 31.1 per cent could not meet the new standard. Rowntree's work was especially important for his emphasis on the three periods of poverty which, typically, inflected working-class life patterns.

Three-quarters of the poverty is due to three causes; 28.6 per cent is due to unemployment, 32.8 per cent to the fact that workers in regular work are not receiving wages sufficiently high to enable them to live above the poverty line, and 14.7 per cent are in poverty on account of old age. Of the income of the families whose poverty is due to unemployment 80 per cent is derived from social services, and 66 per cent is so derived in the case of those whose poverty is due to old age. On the other hand, families whose poverty is due to inadequate wages only derive 1.7 per cent of their total income from social services.

Unemployment

Clearly the only way to overcome poverty in the case of the unemployed is either to find them work or to increase the benefit. Our investigation pointed to the fact that probably about 76 per cent of the unemployed were eagerly seeking for work and capable of working; 12 per cent would need to have their morale restored and their physical condition built up before they were fit for work, while the remainder were people getting on in years, many of whom could only do light work. Some of them were almost past work. If work cannot be found for the unemployed, then, if they are to be raised above the poverty line, the only alternative is to increase benefits.

Inadequate wages

Turning now to the families which are in poverty owing to inadequate wages of the chief wage-earner, notwithstanding the fact that he is in regular work, this is in part due to low wages, in part to large families, and in part to high rents . . .

Of the 1,338 heads of households whose poverty is classified as being due to inadequate wages, 1,157 earned less than 53s. The others were in poverty because wages, although not under 53s., did not suffice to raise them above the poverty line, either because their families were 'large' or their rents were 'high'.

The remedies usually proposed for dealing with poverty due to low wages are statutory minimum wages and family allowances . . . To get rid of it altogether would involve a minimum wage of 53s. a week for an adult male and an allowance of 5s. a week for all dependent children.

Old age

The only way of dealing with poverty due to old age is by increasing the pension, legislation for which is being considered as I write these lines. [*Author's note: Supplementary pensions of up to 9s. a week were granted in 1940 to pensioners who could prove need*.] It is interesting to note that of the 3,268 old age pensioners covered by our schedules only 50 per cent are in poverty. The others either have other sources of income, such as children who are earning money and living at home, or they are themselves living with families who are above the poverty line.

In addition to the old age pensioners covered by our schedules there are probably about 1,700 living with families which are better off than those we investigated, so that probably only 33 per cent of all the old age pensioners in York are living below the poverty line.

The three periods of economic stress

In considering the foregoing facts regarding the number of those in poverty, there is one point which it is important that we should remember, namely, that an investigation such as this one only reveals the conditions at a given moment. There is a constant movement of many families from one class to another according to circumstances. Certainly a number of families remain in one class all their lives – some never rise above the poverty line, some never sink below the richest class – but probably the great majority move, at any rate once, and many more than once, from one class to another, either up or down. The period of greatest economic stress in a working man's life is when he has young children to support, and perhaps the most disturbing fact revealed by this investigation is that *of the working-class children under one year of age 52.5 per cent were found to be living below the poverty line; that 47 per cent would probably remain in poverty for five years or more and 31.5 per cent for ten years or more.* It must, of course, be remembered that not only they but the whole of the families concerned would remain in poverty for these periods. Thus working-class people are liable to be in poverty during childhood and women are liable to be in poverty during the time that they are bearing children. The seriousness of this from the standpoint of the national physique can hardly be overstated. Many are liable to be in poverty again in old age.

(S. B. Rowntree, *Poverty and Progress* (London, Longmans, 1940), pp. 457–9.)

DOCUMENT V The unemployed community

The Pilgrim Trust was founded in 1930 as the result of a financial gift from an American, Edward Stephen Harkness, in recognition of Britain's efforts in the First World War. This study of the long-term unemployed was based on six towns and cities (Blackburn, Leicester, Rhondda, Liverpool, Deptford and Crook, Co. Durham) in order to test the effects of the inequitable distribution of unemployment through the country. The fate of the long-term unemployed (those who had been out of work for twelve months or more) was one of the most worrying aspects of unemployment in the 1930s. There were 480,000 of them in July 1933, and rarely less than 100,000 through most of the 1930s. They proved the most difficult to put back to work, either because their skills had become useless, because they were older than most unemployed, or because they had 'got out of the way of work'.

How much easier it is for an unemployed man who is associated with others like himself to become used to unemployment can be shown by a comparison between the Rhondda and Leicester. If we compare the oldest age group, 55 to 64, in these two places, the difference in 'ease of adjustment' is at once apparent. The long-unemployed man in Leicester of that age is an isolated figure. In the Rhondda he is one of thousands. In the Rhondda it is easy for him to settle down, seeing how many others of his age are forced to do so, and something between a half and two-thirds of the men in this age group had so settled down. In Leicester that was true of about a quarter. In this town more than a fifth could not bring themselves to accept the fact that they would probably never work again, in the Rhondda less than a tenth . . .

. . . In several of the towns visited, the National Unemployed Workers' Movement had representatives, who stood outside the Labour Exchanges, on pay day, collecting a penny a week from the 'dole' money. The sample cases were not asked whether they belonged to it for obvious reasons (as they were not asked anything about their politics), but in a number of instances they volunteered information. One or two had dropped out because they did not think it any use, and there were some criticisms of the local personnel of the Movement, but the majority of those who spoke about it evidently valued it. There can be no doubt, however, that especially in more prosperous places, the tendency of organisations of this kind, as sometimes (although not by any means always) of the unemployed clubs, is with younger men at least to encourage them not to get work.

In places which are less prosperous the unemployed community is less militantly defensive owing to its very size. It is accepted, whereas in prosperous areas the attempt is made to ignore it. In Liverpool there are various reductions in price made for the unemployed and notices appear in the shop-window to that effect. They can get their hair cut cheaper, for instance, and in many places they can get cheaper cinema tickets. On Tyneside some of the unemployed club members get free passes into the cinema as often as three times a week.

(Pilgrim Trust, *Men Without Work* (Cambridge, Cambridge University Press, 1938), pp. 159–63.)

DOCUMENT VI Housing conditions in Manchester

Sir Ernest Simon was a housing expert, the creator of the large Wythenshawe housing estate in Manchester. Here, he and his co-writer described the slum district of Angel Meadow, a jumble of both working and derelict factories – among the working ones a glue factory, which emitted an appalling stench – the skeletons of former warehouses, inhabited and uninhabited houses, a district through which flowed the noisome River Irk.

On a hot summer day existence in the houses nearest it must be almost intolerable.

Apart from the spaces once occupied by houses and now lying absolutely waste, the only playground in the area is that by St. Michael's Church, marked in green on maps, but actually paved with blackened flags. No blade of grass exists in the whole area.

No. 4, F Street. The general appearance and condition of this house inside are very miserable. It is a dark house and the plaster on the passage walls, in particular, was in a bad condition. There is no sink or tap in the house; they are in the small yard, consequently in frosty weather the family is without water. In this house live a man and wife, and seven children, ranging from 15 to 1, and a large, if varying, number of rats.

No 9, B Street. In this house the rain had come through so often that the plaster in one bedroom was bulging dangerously and might have fallen at any time. There were no doors on the bedrooms. Under the window in the front room downstairs mortar had fallen out from between the bricks, so that one could see daylight coming through from the street.

Throughout the areas covered by the surveys, dampness, leaking roofs, peeling plaster and general dilapidation were so common as to be almost a rule; the same can be said regarding infestation with bugs, which is a normal feature of slum houses, and which is practically impossible to deal with in a house which has been infested for years. The fact is that the houses are for the most part completely worn out, and have reached a state when effective repairs are practically impossible.

(E. D. Simon and J. Inman, *The Rebuilding of Manchester* (London, Longman, 1935), p.61.)

DOCUMENT VII Slums and overcrowding in south Wales

Allen Hutt, a historian of the working class in Britain and left-wing activist, made a particular point about the failure of local authorities, for all their building of council houses, to cope with overcrowding and the fact that the very poor could not afford council housing. Here he draws upon the medical officer of health in Swansea, among others, for expert views.

Large numbers of the applicants for Swansea corporation houses were living in seriously overcrowded conditions, many in rooms. On this Dr Evans comments:

> The houses that are sublet for this purpose are without separate family amenities, there is no separate and proper accommodation for cooking, for storage of food, for washing, or separate closet accommodation – and yet – it was estimated that half the applicants for Corporation houses would be unable to pay the rent of a post-war Corporation house.

And in 1929 the medical officer of health in Merthyr was reporting that there was no advance in housing; that there were in the town no fewer than 834 houses which required entire rebuilding to make them habitable; and that 118 cellar-dwellings, many of which had previously been closed, were now each occupied by a separate family, owing to a lack of suitable accommodation. Instances were also given where 'houses that had been closed but not demolished, were broken into and occupied by families who were unable to get housing accommodation. The sanitary circumstances of these houses were deplorable'. And in Dowlais the district sanitary inspector, Mr Jenkins, stated that

'The small number of notices served in this district to reduce overcrowding does not represent the extent of the family over-crowding . . . Owing to the scarcity of suitable accommodation for a large number of families, consisting of young people with two or three children, who now share dwelling-houses by occupying the kitchen cellars, or form one of the families in a large inconvenient house under decidedly unfavourable conditions; only verbal and frequent visits can be brought to bear, and is frequently met with the retort "we cannot find better accommodation or we would soon get out"'.

(A. Hutt, The Condition of the Working Class in Britain (London, Martin Lawrence, 1933), p.35.)

DOCUMENT VIII Food, health and income

Sir John Boyd Orr was already a nutritionist of world stature by the time he came to write this study. Note that nutritionists in this period were clearly not as worried about cholesterol as the nutritionists of later, more sedentary generations were to be! His claims could hardly be dismissed as those of a politically motivated provocateur, though some did suggest that Sir John was offering a counsel of perfection, rather than practicality. Other life scientists such as Julian Huxley, however, were equally damning about what relative poverty did to health. The chance for the state to do something about the national diet came rather sooner than expected. With the coming of the Second World War and the submarine threat in the Atlantic, rationing – based on thorough nutritional research in the Ministry of Food – was to transform equitably the way the nation ate and also to educate widely on the values or dangers of certain foodstuffs. After the war, Boyd Orr became first director general of the United Nations Food and Agriculture Organization. He was given a peerage and won the Nobel Peace Prize in 1949.

I. Of an estimated national income of £3,750 millions, about £1,075 millions are spent on food. This is equivalent to 9s. per head per week.

II. The consumption of bread and potatoes is practically uniform throughout the different income level groups. Consumption of milk, eggs, fruit, vegetables, meat and fish rise with income. Thus, in the poorest group the average consumption of milk, including tinned milk, is equivalent to 1.8 pints per week; in the wealthiest groups 5.5 pints. The poorest group consume 1.5 eggs per head per week; the wealthiest eat 4.5. The poorest spend 2.4d on fruit; the wealthiest 1s 8d.

III. An examination of the composition of the diets of the different groups shows that the degree of adequacy for health increases as income rises. The average diet of the poorest group, comprising 4½ million people, is, by the standard adopted, deficient in every constituent examined. The second group, comprising another 9 million people, is adequate in protein but deficient in all the vitamins and minerals considered. The third group, comprising another 9 million people, is deficient in vitamins and minerals. Complete adequacy is almost reached in group IV, and in the still wealthier groups the diet has a surplus of all constituents considered.

IV. A review of the state of health of the people of the different groups suggests that, as income increases, disease and death-rate decrease, children grow more quickly, adult stature is greater and general health and physique improve.

V. The results of tests on children show that improvement of the diet in the lower groups is accompanied by improvement in health and increased rate of growth, which approximates to that of children in higher income groups.

VI. To make the diet of the poorer groups the same as that of the first group whose diet is adequate for full health, ie group IV, would involve increases in consumption of a number of the more expensive foodstuffs, viz. milk, eggs, butter, fruit, vegetables and meat, varying from 12 to 25 per cent.

If these findings be accepted as sufficiently accurate to form a working hypothesis, they raise important economic and political problems. Consideration of these is outwith the scope of the investigation. It may be pointed out here, however, that one of the main difficulties in dealing with these problems is that they are not within the sphere of any single Department of State. This new knowledge of nutrition, which shows that there can be an enormous improvement in the health and physique of the nation, coming at the same time as the greatly increased powers of producing food, has created an entirely new situation which demands economic statesmanship.

(J. Boyd Orr, *Food, Health and Income* (London, Macmillan, 1937),
pp.55–6.)

DOCUMENT IX Birth control and family life

Marie Stopes published Married Love *in 1918. Her clinics, the first opened in 1921, became important disseminators of information on methods of birth control which, in turn, did much to undercut one major cause of poverty in pre-1914 Britain, over-large families. Although she was considered radical and* risqué *by some sections of opinion, Stopes maintained a strictly conservative moral tone: the emphasis was not on female sexual liberation but on the sanctity of marriage and of motherhood, which methods of birth control were to reinforce, in her view, and in no way challenge. Stopes further publicized her views in the popular periodical* John Bull. *Although Stopes hoped that family planning would make family life blissful, the flood of letters she received provided ample evidence of the undercurrent of continued ignorance which threatened not just family*

life and good health but the very life of so many women, such as this
working-class woman from Norfolk in 1923.

Please could you give me some advice about preventing my self from
becoming pregnant again, I had my first child in 1910 and it was 7
months but after a lot of expense we have managed to rear Him, then
1 year after I was pregnant again and suffered terribly could not get
about by myself after the first month and could do no work and had
a very bad time all through with this awful Pain and after that one
was born could not sit down properly for 7 years, and was doctoring
all the time (and my husband is only a cow-man so its been an awful
drag) at last I went to Hospital and they said I must have an
operation I was in a month and they said I must on no condition
have any more children but did not tell me what to do and the
consequences was I got pregnant again and had an awful time and
the baby had to be removed last March to save my life it lived 7
weeks and died an awful death it lay in agonies for a fortnight, We
tried for it not to happen again but I am now 3 months and having an
awful time, always in pain, and have to diet myself on brown bread,
no Tea and no meat, and I am loosing off and on rather badly I
sometimes bring up blood and when that stops it come the other way
and this last week I have had to keep my feet up as much as possible.
I have gone and tried to end my life and should have done so if my
husband had not prevented me, as it sends me out of my mind with
the pain . . . Trusting you will do your best to help me . . .

(Mrs K.E. to M.C.S., from R. Hall (ed.), *Dear Dr Stopes: Sex in the 1920s*
(London, Deutsch, 1978), p.23.)

DOCUMENT X Child poverty

Herbert Tout found that poverty in Bristol affected virtually the same
proportion of working-class families as Rowntree found for York. The causes
of poverty, moreover, were also virtually identical, although Tout found that
unemployment was a bigger cause of poverty than in York. Tout also isolated
the vicious circle that kept unemployment benefits low, which in turn
allowed low wages to continue for many in employment, a primary cause of
child poverty.

Wages are based on earning power. In turn unemployment benefit
and relief are kept below wages, and so cannot be based entirely on

needs. It is not the stony-heartedness of those responsible for relief that puts unemployment first among the causes of poverty, but their reluctance to upset the delicate balance of the economic system by making relief appear as attractive as work. Thus those who are anxious to find means of combating present distress are faced with a position from which there is no escape so long as the wages of the lower-paid workers will not support more than a small family. This deadlock is responsible for most of the poverty ascribed to unemployment and to insufficient wages, and explains about half of all family poverty. It is responsible for still more child poverty, in fact for about 80 per cent of it . . .

	Percentage of all families below the standard
Unemployment	32.1
Insufficient wages	21.3
Old age	15.2
Absence of adult male earner	13.3
Sickness or incapacity	9.0
Self-employment and hawking	6.5
Other	2.6

(H. Tout, *The Standard of Living in Bristol* (Bristol, Bristol University Press, 1938), pp.45–6.)

DOCUMENT XI *Woman's Own*

One of the major developments in popular publishing in the inter-war years was the range of women's magazines that came onto the market. As well as the relatively expensive monthlies aimed at middle-class women, such as Good Housekeeping *which started in 1922, the latter half of the period saw the development of the weekly magazines aimed at lower middle-class women, such as* Woman's Own, *first published in 1932 with the following introduction.*

How Do You Do?
    We introduce ourselves and our new weekly for the modern young wife who loves her home.

Woman's Own will be a paper with a purpose – a paper thoroughly alive to the altered conditions of the present day. The home paper that makes any girl worth her salt want to be the best housewife ever – and then some.

> (*Woman's Own*, 15 September 1932, in D. Beddoe, *Back to Home and Duty: Women between the Wars* (London, Pandora, 1989), p.14.)

Typically, these magazines featured romantic serials, tips on relatively cheap clothes, advertisements for consumer durables, problem pages featuring readers' letters, and medical advice – especially relating to 'women's problems'. Special emphasis seemed to be placed on a non-specific malady generally known as 'bad nerves'.

Few housewives realise what powers they possess and how much depends on them; how they have within their grasp to make or mar the lives of everyone within the household. They are the pivot – the centre around which this small organisation works and when it is out of gear everything is affected . . . If she takes this nervy condition in hand in its early stages, she will prevent disaster in the future not only from the point of view of her own health, but because she is risking something none of us likes to lose – the power to keep her husband.

> (*Woman's Own*, 31 December 1932, in Beddoe, *Back to Home and Duty: Women between the Wars*, p.111.)

DOCUMENT XII *English Journey*

In the autumn of 1933, J. B. Priestley took himself off on a journey around England. Already established as a popular novelist and playwright, the Bradford-born Priestley projected an avuncular bonhomie, slightly left of centre though hardly radical. First published in 1934, his English Journey *was something of a latter-day* Rural Rides, *almost consciously echoing the journeys made over a century before by William Cobbett. His journey took him through the West Country, Birmingham, Lancashire, Yorkshire and Co. Durham. As he returned home to London, he reckoned that he had seen three Englands: the pretty England of the guidebooks and the cathedrals, the England of the nineteenth century currently so depressed, and the new England which seemed to be the dominant one.*

. . . the new post-war England, belonging far more to the age itself than to this particular island. America, I supposed, was its real birthplace. This is the England of arterial and by-pass roads, of filling stations and factories that look like exhibition buildings, of giant cinemas and dance-halls and cafés, bungalows with tiny garages, cocktail bars, Woolworths, motor-coaches, wireless, hiking, factory girls looking like actresses, greyhound racing and dirt tracks, swimming pools, and everything given away for cigarette coupons. If the fog had lifted I knew that I should have seen this England all around me at that northern entrance to London, where the smooth wide road passes between miles of semi-detached bungalows, all with their little garages, their wireless sets, their periodicals about film stars, their swimming costumes and tennis rackets and dancing shoes . . . I had ample time to consider carefully this newest England, from my richly confused memory of it. Care is necessary too, for you can easily approve or disapprove of it too hastily. It is, of course, essentially democratic. After a social revolution there would, with any luck, be more and not less of it. You need money in this England, but you do not need much money. It is a large-scale, mass-production job, with cut prices. You could almost accept Woolworths as its symbol. Its cheapness is both its strength and its weakness. It is its strength because being cheap it is accessible; it nearly achieves the famous equality of opportunity. In this England, for the first time in history, Jack and Jill are nearly as good as their master and mistress; they may have always been as good in their own way, but now they are nearly as good in the *same way*. Jack, like his master, is rapidly transformed to some place of rather mechanical amusement. Jill beautifies herself exactly as her mistress does. It is an England, at last, without privilege.

(J. B. Priestley, *English Journey* (Harmondsworth, Penguin, 1977), pp.375–6.)

DOCUMENT XIII Cinema audiences

In 1937, the trade journal World Film News *conducted a survey of cinema exhibitors and found that the audience reactions to films split quite clearly into three categories. First, exhibitors showing to working-class audiences were:*

. . . practically unanimous in regarding the majority of British films as unsuitable for their audiences. British films, one Scottish exhibitor writes, should rather be called English films in a particularly parochial sense: they are more foreign to his audience than the products of Hollywood, over 6000 miles away. Again and again exhibitors of this category complain of 'old school tie' standards inherent in so many British films. They describe 'the horse laughs' with which the Oxford accents of supposed crooks are greeted and the impatience of their patrons with the well-worn 'social drama' type of filmed stageshow. Similarly, the lack of action and the excess of superfluous dialogue are censored. A significant statement which frequently occurs, is that English films are too high-brow (in the Bloomsbury sense) or else too stupid for their audiences . . . Films with tempo and action, stirring in their appeal, simple and straightforward in treatment and related to the lives of the people appear to be the type preferred in this group. Comedy and slapstick are also required. Romance and melodrama of the better type are popular, whereas history is almost universally condemned.

Family audiences, on the other hand, preferred:

Light comedy; a simple blending of pathos and humour; romantic films with a sensible story; not too true to life, though dealing with people like themselves whose lives they can understand and whose reactions they can appreciate . . . People in this group want 'something they need not think about, something that will catch the eye, tickle their fancy but not trouble their mind'. Star value is often stated to be particularly important. American films with British actors are most popular, while British films with what are described as 'second-rate stars imported from Hollywood' are deprecated.

Middle-class audiences were looking for something entirely different.

The Gaumont (Matthews–Hitchcock) and Wilcox (Anna Neagle) type of British film seems to go down particularly well. History is often stated to be popular, as are mystery films. American gangster, crime or police films are frowned upon. In the highbrow line popularity seems sometimes, though not equivocally, to extend as far as *Things to Come* . . . As in the former group, star value is stressed, and opinions differ as to whether a single star or a team is the better policy. English actors and backgrounds are favoured even in American films, *Mutiny on the Bounty* being cited as a case in point.

(*World Film News*, 1, 11 (February 1937), pp.6–7, from J. Richards, *The Age of the Dream Palace* (London, Routledge, 1984), pp.24–5.)

DOCUMENT XIV George Formby

Early in his career, Formby adapted from his music-hall star father, George Formby sen., the character of John Willie, with wide-brimmed hat and check jacket, cheeky manner and workshy (and girl-shy) ways. In the film Off the Dole, *he learns from the manager of the Labour Exchange that he is to lose his benefit.*

John Willie. Ay, good morning sir.

Manager. Good morning

John Willie. Good morning

Manager. So, you are John Willie?

John Willie. Yes, so me mother says.

Manager. Hm, well, it's been reported to me that you've been seen working and failed to notify us.

John Willie. What, me working? Get away! Somebody's been kidding yer.

Manager. You were seen yesterday hawking firewood on a handcart.

John Willie. Me, 'awking firewood on 'andcart? Get away, that was our furniture. We were shifting to another address.

Manager. Oh, well, that's different.

John Willie. Aye, clever dick.

Manager. Anyway, what have you been doing for the last four years?

John Willie. Answering questions.

Manager. It seems to me that you're afraid of work.

John Willie. Me, afraid of work? I could sleep beside it.

Manager. Oh, could you?

John Willie. Aye, and when you get me a job, I want a job to me own trade.

Manager. Your own trade?

John Willie. Every man to 'is own trade, I say.

Manager. Well, what is your own trade?

John Willie. Selling calendars every leap year.

Manager. Strikes me that you've got out of the way of work.

John Willie. Well, I've managed it up to now, but it's been a struggle.

Manager. Well, I've got some bad news for you.

John Willie. Nay, they 'aven't found me a job 'ave they?

Manager. No.

John Willie. Yer gave me a fright then, lad.

Manager. They've stopped your dole. In other words, you're off the dole.

John Willie. Off the dole?

Manager. Yes. Off the dole.

John Willie. Eh! fancy 'em knocking me off the dole, and I've been one of yer best customers. Aye, it's alright shrugging yer shoulders. That's what you get for giving the best years of your life. I want a reason, now come on.

Manager. You've had quite sufficient reason. You haven't tried hard enough to find work.

(Dialogue from *Off the Dole*, Mancunian Films, 1935.)

DOCUMENT XV On England

Stanley Baldwin liked to appeal above politics to a historical sense of Englishness, which he equated with the countryside. It was almost as if he were suggesting that the trials and tribulations of urban, industrial England had nothing to do with the real nation that went on under the surface.

To me, England is the country, and the country is England. And when I ask myself what I mean by England, when I think of England when I am abroad, England comes to me through my various senses through the ear, through the eye, and through certain imperishable scents. I will tell you what they are, and there may be those among you who feel as I do.

The sounds of England, the tinkle of the hammer on the anvil in the country smithy, the corncrake on a dewy morning, the sounds of the scythe against the whetstone, and the sight of a plough team coming over the brow of a hill, the sight that has been seen in England since England was a land, and may be seen in England long after the Empire has perished and every works in England has ceased to function, for centuries the one eternal sight of England. The wild anemones in the woods in April, the last load at night of hay being drawn down a lane as the twilight comes on, when you can scarcely distinguish the figures of the horses as they take it home to the farm, and above all, most subtle, most penetrating and most moving, the smell of wood smoke coming up in an autumn evening, or the smell of the scutch fires: that wood smoke that our ancestors, tens of thousands of years ago, must have caught on the air when they were coming home with the result of the day's forage, when they were still nomads, and when they were still roaming the forests and plains of the continent of Europe. These things strike down into the very depths of our nature, and touch chords that go back to the beginning of time and the human race, but they are chords that with every year of our life sound a deeper note in our innermost beings.

These are the things that make England, and I grieve for it that they are not the childish inheritance of the majority of the people today in our country. They ought to be the inheritance of every child born into this country, but nothing can be more touching than to see how the working man and woman after generations in the towns will have their tiny bit of garden if they can, will go to gardens it they can, to look at something they have never seen as children, but which their ancestors knew and loved. The love of these things is innate and inherent in our people. It makes for that love of home, one of the strongest features of our race, and it is this that makes our race seek its new home in the Dominions overseas, where they have room to see things like this that they can no more see at home. It is that power of making homes, almost peculiar to our people, and it is one of the sources of their greatness. They go overseas, and they take with them what they learned at home: love of justice, love of truth and the broad humanity that are so characteristic of English people.

(S. Baldwin, *On England* (Harmondsworth, Penguin, 1938), pp.14–15.)

DOCUMENT XVI The prime minister speaks out

The Conservative party carefully courted the newsreel companies and, as a result, were given glorious opportunities for propaganda. Here Stanley Baldwin was caught apparently at his desk in 10 Downing Street, talking directly to camera and apparently without script, He advanced the line which he had made central to post-1918 Conservative ideology, congratulating the audience on being British, fair-minded, consensual and moderate.

When we read of conditions and events in the world around us, I think we must all be filled with a sense of profound thankfulness that we are living in this country under a system of national government. In many countries abroad we see fears and suspicions, economic and industrial depression, the destruction of liberty and freedom, conscription on an increasing scale, violence and disturbance, and in

Spain we witness the climax in the terrible horrors of civil war. Contrast these conditions with the peace and prosperity of our own country. For five years we have enjoyed an economic recovery which is still continuing. In the first nine months of this year employment increased by well over half a million. For two years the level of wages has been constantly rising. Many industries are breaking all previous records in production. I know the difficulties that still remain in some districts, but all over the country our social services are expanding, and I believe it is true to say that there never has been a time in our history when the people as a whole have been more prosperous, better cared for and more contented. What is the reason for this remarkable contrast? It can be summed up in one word – confidence: confidence in industry, confidence in finance, and confidence in one another. This confidence is largely due to the fact that, when our country was faced with crisis, there were men of all parties who put party politics on one side and united together to pull the country through and to take the necessary steps to put our finances once more on a sound basis. But it is also due to the fact that we, as a nation true to our old traditions, have avoided all extremes. We have steered clear of fascism, communism, dictatorship, and we have shown the world that democratic government, constitutional methods and ordered liberty are not inconsistent with progress and prosperity.

('The prime minister speaks out', *Gaumont British News*, 21 November 1936, reproduced on InterUniversity History Film Consortium videocassette, Archive Series, *Stanley Baldwin*.)

DOCUMENT XVII United for action

The Times *here sets out the charges that were to be levelled against the Labour party after 1931. While Labour was to complain about the 'great betrayal' of MacDonald and Snowden, while they suspected a 'bankers' ramp', the right accused Labour of running away from a crisis and kowtowing to the opinion of the TUC, rather than putting the interest of the country first.*

The country awakens this morning to find Mr MacDonald still Prime Minister, with the prospect of a small Cabinet representative of all three parties. The former Cabinet resigned yesterday afternoon, and a statement issued last night announced that considerable progress had been made towards settling the composition of its successor, which would be a Government of co-operation formed for the specific purposes only of carrying through a very large reduction of expenditure and raising 'on an equitable basis' the further funds required to balance the Budget. On Sunday night it had already become clear that the courageous determination of Mr MacDonald and Mr Snowden to adopt a policy of retrenchment, including especially cuts in the dole, had cleft an unbridgeable gulf between two sections in the Socialist Cabinet; but it was not until yesterday morning that a salutary and steadying announcement from Buckingham Palace revealed that the leaders of all three parties, having been summoned to visit the King, were considering the formation of a National Government.

All concerned are to be warmly congratulated on this result, so fully in accord with the patriotic spirit which has inspired a week's most anxious negotiations. The Prime Minister and the colleagues of his own party who have followed him deserve in particular unqualified credit, both for the manner in which they took their political lives in their hands and forcing the break-up of the late Cabinet, and for their new decision to translate courage in the Cabinet into courage in the country. Their readiness to share the responsibility – honour is perhaps the better word – of carrying through to the end a policy of retrenchment adds enormously to the prospect of its success. No one henceforth will ever be able to claim that retrenchment is a class or partisan policy, dictated solely by an insubstantial panic manufactured by industrial and financial interests . . .

It is an interesting, dramatic, and logical fact that the Labour Government has fallen in what has always been foreseen to be the acid test of democracy – namely, the capacity of its leaders to tell the people the truth and not to regulate their policy by the votes that it would bring. That is the test which Mr MacDonald, Mr Snowden, and those who supported them have triumphantly survived. That is the test to which their dissentient colleagues have ingloriously succumbed. The secessionists are frankly those who dare not stand on a platform and expound a policy which they know to be necessary to the country. The proposal against which they rebelled was to fix the rate of unemployment benefit at a real value of over 2s. a week more than in 1928 and of over 4s. more than they themselves tolerated in 1924. That proposal was an ineradicable part of the minimum necessary to restore confidence in sterling. It is understood that the original scheme approved by the whole Socialist

Cabinet for submission to the Opposition parties and to the TUC contained measures at least equally drastic. The rebellion of the dissentients is therefore nothing less than ignominious, because it clearly originated in opposition manifested outside the Cabinet.

('United for action', *The Times*, 25 August 1931, p.13.)

DOCUMENT XVIII The chiefs of staff and Czechoslovakia

In the late summer of 1938 the chiefs of staff, the uniformed heads of the three armed services, were asked to give their estimate of the military situation which would arise if Britain went to war with Germany over Czechoslovakia. Although the printed final version of this paper did not appear until after the crisis had been defused at the Munich conference, the Cabinet had read earlier typed drafts.

We have been instructed to prepare, as a matter of urgency, an up-to-date appreciation showing the situation which will arise in the event of our being involved in immediate hostilities against Germany.

2. We have made the following political ... assumptions as basis for our appreciation:

3. (A) Political Assumptions

(i) The basis of the present Appreciation is that we should be drawn into hostilities as a result of German aggression against Czechoslovakia, since this would lead to intervention first by France and then by ourselves.

(ii) Italy might combine with Germany against us from the outset, or she might await some clarification of the military situation before she commits herself indefinitely. Our initial dispositions, with particular reference to the Eastern Mediterranean, must be framed to meet the former eventuality. Such dispositions will place us in a better position to influence Italy's attitude, and possibly to deter her from joining Germany.

(iii) Japanese operations in China continue to absorb a considerably greater proportion of her land forces and economic strengths than she probably anticipated. Nevertheless, there are undoubted indications that Japan may avail herself of a good opportunity to further her ambitions in the Far East at our expense. We must therefore assume Japan to be potentially hostile.

(iv) The United States of America, despite an appreciable movement of informed opinion away from isolation, cannot be relied upon to come to our assistance.

(v) The attitude of the USSR is incalculable, and it is unsafe to assume that Soviet Russia would go to the assistance of Czechoslovakia.

(vi) Palestine already absorbs a considerable military force, and the local authorities have asked for further reinforcements. There is a danger that the infection of lawlessness may spread to neighbouring Mohammedan countries. Consequently, Iraq, Saudi Arabia, and the Yemen, and perhaps also Persia, must for some time to come be regarded as uncertain friends.

(vii) Franco Spain is likely to be sympathetic towards Germany, and may be expected to afford port facilities which would be of value to Germany's naval forces attacking our trade routes.

(viii) The remaining countries in the world, with the exception of Portugal and Egypt, are assumed to be initially neutral.

After surveying other factors involved, and possible courses of action by both sides, the chiefs of staff concluded:

29. It is our opinion that no pressure that Great Britain and France can bring to bear, either by sea, on land, or in the air, could prevent Germany from overrunning Bohemia and from inflicting a decisive defeat on Czechoslovakia. The restoration of Czechoslovakia's lost integrity could only be achieved by the defeat of Germany and as the outcome of a prolonged struggle, which from the outset must assume the character of an unlimited war.

30. The intervention of Italy and/or Japan on the side of Germany would create a situation which the Chiefs of Staff in their 'Mediterranean and Middle East Appreciation', described in the following language:

> Moreover, war against Japan, Germany and Italy simultaneously in 1938 is a commitment which neither the present nor the projected strength of our defence forces is designed to meet, even if they were in alliance with France and Russia, and which would, therefore, place a dangerous strain on the resources of the Empire . . .

(Public Record Office, London: COS765, 'Appreciation of the situation in the event of war with Germany', 4 October 1938.)

Bibliography

Historians and the depression

Texts mentioned in the chapter are: A. J. P. Taylor, *English History, 1914–1945* (Harmondsworth, Penguin, 1970); Cato, *Guilty Men* (London, Gollancz, 1940); Malcolm Muggeridge, *The Thirties* (London, Weidenfeld and Nicolson, 1940); Robert Graves and Alan Hodge, *The Long Weekend: A Social History of Great Britain, 1918–1939* (London, Faber, 1940); W. S. Churchill, *The Second World War*, vol.1 (London, Cassell, 1948); George Orwell, 'My country right or left', in *Collected Essays, Journalism and Letters*, vol.1 (Harmondsworth, Penguin, 1968); C. L. Mowat, *Britain Between the Wars, 1918–1940* (London, Methuen, 1955); A. Marwick, 'Middle opinion in the thirties', *English Historical Review*, vol.79, 1964; A. Marwick, *Britain in the Age of Total War* (Harmondsworth, Penguin, 1968); A. J. P. Taylor, *The Origins of the Second World War* (Harmondsworth, Penguin, 1961); Martin Gilbert and Richard Gott, *The Appeasers* (London, Weidenfeld and Nicolson, 1967); Angus Calder, *The People's War* (London, Cape, 1969); Margot Heinemann and Noreen Branson, *Britain in the 1930s* (St Albans, Panther, 1973); D. Aldcroft and H. W. Richardson, *The British Economy, 1870–1939* (London, Macmillan, 1969); Sean Glynn and John Oxborrow, *Interwar Britain: An Economic and Social History* (London, Allen and Unwin, 1976); Chris Cook and John Stevenson, *The Slump: Society and Politics during the Depression* (London, Cape, 1978); Keith Middlemas and John Barnes, *Baldwin: A Biography* (London, Weidenfeld and Nicolson, 1969); G. M. Young, *Stanley Baldwin* (London, Hart Davis, 1952); David Marquand, *Ramsay MacDonald* (London, Cape, 1977); R. P. Shay, *British Rearmament in the Thirties* (Princeton, Princeton University Press, 1977); George Peden, *British Rearmament and the Treasury* (Edinburgh, Scottish University Press, 1979); Paul Kennedy, *The Realities behind*

Diplomacy: Background Influences on British External Policy (London, Fontana, 1981); R. A. C. Parker, *Chamberlain and Appeasement: British Policy and the Coming of the Second World War* (London, 1993); Correlli Barnett, *The Audit of War: The Illusion and Reality of Britain as a Great Nation* (London, Macmillan, 1986); John Charmley, *Chamberlain and the Lost Peace* (London, Hodder and Stoughton, 1991); John Charmley, *Churchill: The End of Glory* (London, Hodder and Stoughton, 1993); Jeffrey Richards, *The Age of the Dream Palace: Cinema and Society in Britain 1930–1939* (London, Routledge and Kegan Paul, 1984); Peter Stead, *Film and the Working Class: The Feature Film in British and American Society* (London, Routledge, 1989); Paddy Scannell and David Cardiff, *Social History of Broadcasting* (Oxford, Blackwell, 1991); John Baxendale and Christopher Pawling, *Narrating the Thirties. A Decade in the Making: 1930 to the Present* (London, Macmillan, 1996).

Other general works which set the period in context include Keith Laybourn, *Britain on the Breadline: A Social and Political History of Britain between the Wars* (Gloucester, Alan Sutton, 1990); K. G. Robbins, *The Eclipse of a Great Power: Modern Britain, 1870–1992* (London, Longman, 1994); Malcolm Smith, *British Politics, Society and the State since the Late Nineteenth Century* (Basingstoke, Macmillan, 1990) and Peter Dewey, *War and Progress: Britain, 1914–1945* (London, Longman, 1997). The heroic socialist view of the inter-war period can still be found, for instance in Nigel Gray, *The Worst of Times: An Oral History of the Great Depression in Britain* (London, Wildwood House, 1985). Frequently reissued and an important general survey of England in this century is T. O. Lloyd, *Empire, Welfare State, Europe: English History 1906–1992*, 4th edn (Oxford, Oxford University Press, 1993).

The economy: the end of British hegemony

Derek Aldcroft has made a number of important contributions to the economic history of inter-war Britain since his early work with Harry Richardson. Notable among these are: D. H. Aldcroft, *The Inter-War Economy: Britain, 1919–1939* (London, Batsford, 1970); *The British Economy between the Wars* (Oxford, Philip Allan, 1983); *The British Economy*, vol.1: *The Years of Turmoil 1920–1951* (Brighton, Wheatsheaf, 1986); and, with Neil Buxton, *British Industry between the Wars: Instability and Industrial Development, 1919–1939* (London,

Scolar Press, 1979). Sean Glynn and Alan Booth also continue to contribute substantially, as in their *Modern Britain: An Economic and Social History* (London, Routledge, 1996). Another important general work is B. W. E. Alford, *Britain in the World Economy since 1880* (London, Longman, 1996).

There is an important set of statistics on the inter-war economy in Forrest Capie and Michael Collins, *The Inter-War British Economy: A Statistical Abstract* (Manchester, Manchester University Press, 1983). See also Forrest Capie, *Depression and Protectionism: Britain between the Wars* (London, Allen and Unwin, 1983). A sophisticated analysis is to be found in S. N. Broadberry, *The British Economy Between the Wars: A Macroeconomic Survey* (Oxford, Blackwell, 1986). The importance of female workers to the new industries is discussed in Miriam Glucksmann, *Women Assemble: Women Workers and the New Industries in Inter-War Britain* (London, Routledge, 1990). For more on the new consumer economy, see John Benson, *The Rise of Consumer Society in Britain, 1880–1980* (London, Longman, 1994). For more on women workers, see also T. J. Hatton, *Female Labour Force Participation: The Enigma of the Interwar Period* (London, Centre for Economic Policy Research, 1986).

On Keynes, see D. E. Moggridge, *Keynes* (Basingstoke, Macmillan, 1980). Some Labour thinking on economics is detailed in Noel W. Thompson, *Political Economy and the Labour Party: The Economics of Democratic Socialism, 1884–1995* (London, UCL Press, 1996). The Tories' problems with tariff policy are covered in Robert C. Self, *Tories and Tariffs: The Conservative Party and the Politics of Tariff Reform, 1922–1932* (New York, Garland, 1986).

Society and the state

The slightly contentious book mentioned in the text is Bentley Gilbert, *British Social Policy, 1914–1939* (London, Batsford, 1970). Not only is it contentious, it is also now rather dated. One of the most important newer works on inter-war society is Keith Laybourn, *Britain on the Breadline: A Social and Political History of Britain between the Wars* (Gloucester, Alan Sutton, 1990). John Stevenson, *Social Conditions in Britain between the Wars* (Harmondsworth, Penguin, 1977) provides a useful number of lengthy extracts from the inter-war social investigators. See also Stevenson's *British Society, 1914–45* (Harmondsworth, Penguin, 1984). A. H. Halsey, *Trends in British*

Society since 1900 (Basingstoke, Macmillan, 1972), is very useful for statistics which allow the inter-war period to be put into perspective. Also useful for seeing the significance of these years in a longer time-span is Kathleen Jones, *The Making of Social Policy in Britain, 1830–1990*, 2nd edn (London, Athlone, 1994).

See Christopher Grayling, *A Land Fit for Heroes? Life in England after the Great War* (London, Buchan and Enright, 1986), and L. C. B. Seaman, *Life in Britain between the Wars* (London, Batsford, 1985). Stephen Constantine, *Social Conditions in Britain, 1918–1939* (London, Methuen, 1983), is only forty-odd pages long but a masterpiece of economy, a model of its kind. Working-class spending patterns are studied in Paul Johnson, *Saving and Spending: The Working-Class Economy in Britain 1870–1939* (Oxford, Clarendon, 1985). For the Welsh experience, see Trevor Herbert and Gareth Elwyn Jones, *Wales between the Wars* (Cardiff, University of Wales Press, 1988).

On a more general level, there are James Hadfield, *Evolution of British Economy and Society, 1870–1979* (Worthing, Churchman, 1990), and Martin Pugh, *State and Society: British Political and Social History, 1870–1992* (Oxford, Edward Arnold, 1994).

Cultures: leisure in the depression

Boris Ford (ed.), *The Cambridge Cultural History of Britain*, Vol.8: *Early Twentieth Century Britain* (Cambridge, Cambridge University Press, 1992), deals very adequately with the high culture of the period. It may usefully be compared with the issues raised in Frank Gloversmith (ed.), *Class, Culture, and Social Change: A New View of the 1930s* (Brighton, Harvester, 1980), or Peter Miles and Malcolm Smith, *Cinema, Literature and Society: Élite and Mass Culture in Interwar Britain* (London, Croom Helm, 1987).

For issues of gender and domesticity, see Deidre Beddoe, *Back to Home and Duty: Women Between the Wars, 1918–1939* (London, Pandora, 1989), Joanna Bourke, *Working Class Cultures in Britain, 1890–1960: Gender, Class, and Ethnicity* (London, Routledge, 1994), and also Sybil Oldfield, *This Working-Day World: Women's Lives and Culture(s) in Britain, 1914–1945* (London, Taylor and Francis, 1994). On sport, there are Derek Birley, *Playing the Game: Sport and British Society, 1914–1945* (Manchester, Manchester University Press, 1995), and Stephen G. Jones, *Sport, Politics and the Working Class:*

Organised Labour and Sport in Inter-War Britain (Manchester, Manchester University Press, 1988). The new interest in the countryside of the period is covered in John Sheail, *Rural Conservation in Inter-War Britain* (Oxford, Clarendon, 1981).

The culture of the radicalized working class is the subject of Stuart Macintyre, *Little Moscows: Communism and Working-Class Militancy in Inter-War Britain* (London, Croom Helm, 1980), while some of the cultural issues surrounding social class are tackled in Arthur Marwick, *Class: Image and Reality in Britain, France and the USA since 1930*, 2nd edn (Basingstoke, Macmillan, 1990).

For inter-war cinema, there is simply no substitute for Jeffrey Richards, *The Age of the Dream Palace: Cinema and Society in Britain 1930–1939* (London, Routledge and Kegan Paul, 1984), but see also Jeffrey Richards and Anthony Aldgate, *Best of British: Cinema and Society 1930–1970* (Oxford, Blackwell, 1983), and Peter Stead, *Film and the Working Class: The Feature Film in British and American Society* (London, Routledge, 1989).

There is also an interesting discussion of the forging of identities in Eugenio F. Biagini (ed.), *Citizenship and Community: Liberals, Radicals, and Collective Identities in the British Isles, 1865–1931* (Cambridge, Cambridge University Press, 1996), while young people are covered in David Fowler, *The First Teenagers: The Lifestyle of Young Wage-Earners in Interwar Britain* (London, Woburn, 1995).

Some of the contemporary journalistic pieces and novels mentioned in the text are still available, notably J. B. Priestley, *English Journey* (London, Heinemann, 1934, repr. Harmondsworth, Penguin, 1977), Lewis Grassic Gibbon, *A Scots Quair* (London, Hutchinson, 1946, repr. 1983), Walter Greenwood, *Love on the Dole* (London, Cape, 1933, repr. Harmondsworth, Penguin, 1971), George Orwell, *The Road to Wigan Pier* (London, Gollancz, 1937, repr. Harmondsworth, Penguin, 1971). There are also some copies still around of Bert Coombs, *These Poor Hands* (London, Gollancz, 1939).

The structure of politics

While virtually no political historian was interested in the Tories in the 1970s, the Conservative ascendancy under Margaret Thatcher seemed to lead to a plethora of studies of the party. Chief among these are: Stuart Ball, *Baldwin and the Conservative Party: The Crisis of 1929–1931* (New Haven, Yale University Press, 1988); Stuart Ball,

The Conservative Party and British Politics, 1902–1951 (London, Longman, 1995); Anthony Seldon and Stuart Ball (eds.), *Conservative Century: The Conservative Party since 1900* (Oxford, Oxford University Press, 1994); Martin Pugh, *The Tories and the People 1880–1935* (Oxford, Blackwell, 1985); Duncan Watts, *Stanley Baldwin and the Search for Consensus* (London, Hodder and Stoughton, 1996); Robert C. Self, *Tories and Tariffs: The Conservative Party and the Politics of Tariff Reform, 1922–1932* (New York, Garland, 1986); Jeremy Smith, *The Taming of Democracy: The Conservative Party, 1880–1924* (Cardiff, University of Wales Press, 1997). Slightly older, but very useful, is John Ramsden, *The Age of Balfour and Baldwin, 1902–1940* (London, Longman, 1978). There are a number of biographies of Baldwin. See especially Keith Middlemas and John Barnes, *Baldwin: A Biography* (London, Weidenfeld and Nicolson, 1969), and Roy Jenkins, *Baldwin* (London, Papermac, 1995).

For the Labour Party, see Keith Burgess, *The Challenge of Labour: Shaping British Society, 1850–1930* (London, Croom Helm, 1980); F. M. Leventhal, *Arthur Henderson* (Manchester, Manchester University Press, 1989); Andrew Thorpe, *A History of the British Labour Party* (London, Macmillan, 1997); Robert D. Pearce, *Attlee* (London, Longman, 1997); Noel W. Thompson, *Political Economy and the Labour Party: The Economics of Democratic Socialism, 1884–1995* (London, UCL Press, 1996); Keith Laybourn, *The Rise of Labour: The British Labour Party 1890–1979: Problems and Perspectives of Interpretation* (London, Edward Arnold, 1988); James D. Young, *Socialism and the English Working Class: A History of English Labour, 1883–1939* (New York, Harvester Wheatsheaf, 1989). The decline of the Liberal Party in this period can be traced in Paul Adelman, *The Decline of the Liberal Party, 1910–1931*, 2nd edn (London, Longman, 1995); G. R. Searle, *The Liberal Party: Triumph and Disintegration, 1886–1929* (Basingstoke, Macmillan, 1992); Chris Cook, *A Short History of the Liberal Party, 1900–92*, 4th edn (Basingstoke, Macmillan, 1993). For a study of those outside the mainstream of politics, see Andrew Thorpe (ed.), *The Failure of Political Extremism in Inter-War Britain* (Exeter, University of Exeter Press, 1989).

The policy of appeasement has been exhaustively researched. A good starting-point might be K. G. Robbins, *Appeasement*, 2nd edn (Oxford, Blackwell, 1997). There is a useful selection of points of view in Patrick Finney (ed.), *Great Britain and the Origins of the Second World War* (London, Edward Arnold, 1997). See also Richard Cockett, *Twilight of Truth: Chamberlain, Appeasement, and the*

Manipulation of the Press (London, Weidenfeld and Nicolson, 1989); Ronald Cameron, *Appeasement and the Road to War* (Glasgow, Pulse, 1991); R. J. Q. Adams (ed.), *British Appeasement and the Origins of World War II* (Lexington, Mass., D. C. Heath, 1994). Not to be missed is R. A. C. Parker, *Chamberlain and Appeasement: British Policy and the Coming of the Second World War* (London, Macmillan, 1993).

Index